HEAVEN AND CHARING CROSS

Edmund Banyard

But (when so sad thou canst not sadder)
Cry; – and upon thy so sore loss
Shall shine the traffic of Jacob's ladder
Pitched betwixt Heaven and Charing Cross.

Francis Thompson
from *The Kingdom of God*

A further collection of meditations and prayers based on the Lectionary

NCEC

Other books by Edmund Banyard published by NCEC:

The Flame
A Fistful of Fivers
A Packet of Crackers
The Maker Of Things
(with Graham Bishop-Hunt)
Turn But A Stone

Cover design:
Peggy Chapman

Text illustrations:
One and a Half Graphics, Caterham, Surrey
and Wendy Carolan

Published by:
National Christian Education Council
1020 Bristol Road
Selly Oak
Birmingham
B29 6LB

British Library Cataloguing in Publication Data:
A catalogue record for this book is available from the British Library.

ISBN 0-7197-0886-9

First published 1996
© Edmund Banyard 1996

Typeset by National Christian Education Council.
Printed and bound by BPCC–AUP Aberdeen Ltd.

Contents

Contents

Preface

e meditations, lyrics, prose passages and prayers in *Heaven And Charing Cross* have en brought together within the framework of the Christian Year following the lec- nary (*JLG2*) of the Joint Liturgical Group to form a volume which, whilst complete in elf, complements *Turn But A Stone* which follows the same pattern.

e liturgical calendar makes a useful framework and this particular lectionary, covering it does a four-year cycle, has provided the stimulation of a broad range of themes. The tionary is however only a stalking-horse, and the outline and indices are intended to nplify the use of material at other times and in other ways. In particular an index of olical references should facilitate the use of *Heaven And Charing Cross* by those who e not using this particular lectionary.

nas been encouraging to learn that *Turn But A Stone* has proved useful in private as ll as corporate prayer. *Heaven And Charing Cross* is offered in the same way for use th at home and in public worship.

me pieces have been published previously, particularly in *All Year Round* (CCBI). nere they are extracted from a larger work, the source is indicated.

mund Banyard
ss, Norfolk
96

Abbreviations and Acknowledgements

We are grateful for permission to quote from the following Bible versions:

AV	Authorised Version
GNB	Good News Bible
REB	Revised English Bible © Oxford University ar Cambridge University Presses, 1989.
RSV	Revised Standard Version
JB	Jerusalem Bible

The compiler and publishers express thanks for permission to use copyright items. Eve effort has been made to trace copyright owners but if any rights have been inadverter ly overlooked, the necessary corrections will gladly be made in subsequent editions.

The copyright for the following items is held by Stainer and Bell Ltd and they are us with permission.

Page

58	'Wake me Lord'
92	'Over to You – a dialogue'
102	'A light beyond the darkness'
	are all from the play *Out Of This World*.

61	'Horses and chariots of fire'
105	'Safely dead, the prophet may be honoured'
112	'Few trippers came to see the stone'
144	'How shall we who are engaged in conflict'
	first appeared in the anthology *Prophets in Action*.

69	'One Friday in Eternity'
77	'A carpenter speaks'
	are from the play *One Friday In Eternity*.

89	'Lord, help us to know joy'
	first appeared in the anthology *Word Alive*.

135	'How shall you value the life of a man'
139	'I haven't got a song for the charts'
	are from the play *The Battle*.

The copyright of the following items remains with the author:

31	'Light the beacon' is from the musical play *George* published by RADIUS.
133	'You will have no easy living' is from the musical play *Ragman* based on Paul's experience in Ephesus, produced at the Westminster Theatre, 1980.
164	'Holy is the soil' is from *The Maker of Things* published by NCEC.

So Many Things I Can't Believe

9th before christmas

He exists before all things, and all things are held together in him.
Colossians 1:17 REB

Fools say to themselves, 'There is no God'.
Psalm 14.1 (Psalm 53.1) GNB

There are so many things
I can't believe.

I can't believe
the universe
exists purely by chance,
without plan,
design
or purpose.

I can't believe
the sum of human history
is nothing but struggle,
where those best able to adapt
to changing circumstances
survive,
procreate
and die.

I can't believe
all striving after truth and beauty
is meaningless
– no moral values;
– no evil to be resisted;
– no good to be won.

I can't believe
all love,
compassion
and self-sacrifice
can be explained away
in purely biological terms.

I stand where
every human being stands,
on the edge of mystery,
– unfathomed depths
– unscaled heights
– great burning questions
– vast unknowns ...
... but still
I cannot
not believe
in God.

So Many Things I Can't Believe

Blessed be God,
whose ways
are far beyond our ways;
whose truth
is so much greater than our truth;
whose wisdom
cannot be comprehended by our knowledge;
whose love
is the origin and renewal of all love
and whose life
is the source of all life.
Blessed be God.

A Better World?

9th before Christmas

Then the Lord answered Job out of the tempest: ...Where were you when I laid the earth's foundations?

Job 38.1,4 REB

Surely there's a fault
at the heart of creation;
it must have been possible
to make a better world;
a world without earthquakes,
volcanoes, floods or famines;
a world without disease,
hunger, pain or sorrow;
without predators
and prey.
What sort of God
could make
such a world as this?

I don't understand
why things are as they are;
there are too many questions
for which I have no answer.
Yet ...

I am held
by the Gospel faith
that God, the Creator,
is in the world with us;
committed to us;
sharing our joys and our sorrows;
sharing our weakness and our pain
to the death –
and then still with us
in the life
which lies
beyond the death.

> **When all is dark**
> **and doubts are magnified;**
> **when faith grows weak**
> **and I relax**
> **my hold on you;**
> **Lord, in your mercy**
> **and the greatness of your love,**
> **do not loose your hold on me.**

3

Beyond The Known

**8th
before
Christmas**

*What is a frail mortal, that you should be mindful of him, a human being
that you should take notice of him?*

Psalm 8.4 REB

I do not know what I may appear to the world, but to myself I seem to have be
only a boy playing on the sea-shore, and diverting myself in now and then fir
ing a smoother pebble or a prettier shell than ordinary, whilst the great ocean
truth lay all undiscovered before me.

Isaac Newton, Brewster's Memoirs of Newt

Not one amazing universe
but many;
expanding,
contracting,
with distances
and time-scales
beyond the ability
of my mind to comprehend –
Can this really be?

And is it true
that 'solid matter'
is not solid,
but all is pulsing energy?

Before these
and other mysteries
how can I stand
except in awe,
wonder and amazement,
when science,
its frontiers ever expanding,
has rediscovered
humility?

Age follows age,
mountains rise
and are worn away,
ice sheets come and go
and humanity
is a very late comer
to an ever-changing world
in an ever-changing universe,
where there is only one constant –
the God
in whom we live and move
and have our being.

Beyond The Known

This is how we know what love is: Christ gave his life for us.

1 John 3.16 REB

**Ever-fashioning,
ever-renewing God;
may we never lose
our sense of awe,
wonder
and sheer amazement
at this universe
of which we are
so insignificant a part.
Yet may we never be so overawed
that we forget
that great as you are,
and vast and intricate
as are your works,
you know and love
each one of us,
and we are ever in your care.**

Far Too Sophisticated?

8th before Christmas

He makes ... an image to which he bows down and prostrates himself; he prays to it and says, 'Save me; for you are my god.'

Isaiah 44.17 REB

Declaration

Idols?
Not us, Lord,
no time for idols
or any of that nonsense,
we're far too sophisticated;
wouldn't think of it:
in fact, to be perfectly honest,
we haven't much time
for religion at all these days,
we've grown out of it, you know;
we don't even need YOU any longer.

Response

So you think you are different
from earlier generations,
so mature
that you no longer need me?
Then why do you study horoscopes
and reverence opinion polls?
Why do you worship money,
possessions, power and prestige?
Do you not see
that you are great idolaters?
What will you do when,
with idolaters of every age,
you learn at last
that there is no hope,
no salvation,
except in the living God?

**When we chase after false gods,
open our eyes to our follies
that we may see what we are really doing;
and in your mercy, Lord, forgive us,
and bring us back to yourself;
for in you alone can we find
the security we so desire.**

Is There A God Who Listens?

7th before

It cannot be that God's word has proved false.

Romans 9.6 REB

I have been young and now have grown old, but never have I seen the righteous forsaken or their children begging bread.

Psalm 37.25 REB

That psalmist must have led
a singularly sheltered life;
with such a simplistic view
of rewards and punishments;
and the belief
that you only suffered
if you deserved it.

The writer
of the book of Job
plumbs greater depths –
crying out against unmerited suffering
and refusing to be silenced.

I still rebel and complain against God; I can't hold back my groaning. How I wish I knew where to find him, and knew how to go where he is.

Job 23.2-3 GNB

Jesus told the story
of an unworthy judge
who reluctantly
gave a persistent claimant justice,
just to stop her worrying him any further
and he added ...

Then will not God give justice to his chosen, to whom he listens patiently while they cry out to him day and night? I tell you, he will give them justice soon enough. But when the Son of Man comes, will he find faith on earth?

Luke 18.7-8 REB

Though suffering is added to suffering,
injustice to injustice
and there are still no easy answers
to the question 'Why?';
Lord, may I never
lose my faith
that you
do hear,
do care,
and do reach out to us
in strong, enfolding love.

Faith And Action
(An Intercession)

7th before Christmas

So with faith; if it does not lead to action, it is by itself a lifeless thing.
James 2.17 REB

Heavenly Father,
we lift up to you those of our dear friends
who have special needs at this time.
Some are lonely;
some are sad;
some have to fight daily battles with sickness;
some are faced with difficult decisions;
some are finding themselves stretched
to the very limits of their endurance.
We pray that even in their darkest moments
they may know that they are loved;
loved by us,
and loved by you.
May they be able to feel
the warmth of that love
and find in it comfort and strength.

We think of others whom you love
and bid us to love
for your sake.
Some are homeless;
some are mentally or physically disabled;
some have never known a happy home life;
some are embittered and angry,
seeing the world about them as full of enemies.
We pray for them.
We confess the injustices in our society
which contribute to their ills.
Lord, help us to care more deeply
for those less fortunate than ourselves,
and help us to express that care
in worthy actions.

In the wider world we pray for
– those who only know extreme poverty;
– those dying of starvation;
– those who suffer from the breakdown of law and order;
– those caught up in war or the threat of war.

Faith And Action
(An Intercession)

Help us and all Christian people
to take more seriously
our calling to be
messengers of peace and reconciliation,
instruments through which
your love may be expressed
to the neediest of your children.

Never allow us to forget
that we are at all times
in your keeping;
strengthen us when our faith falters
and lead us
in caring and compassionate ways,
that wherever we go,
something of your loving care
may go with us.

Beyond Language

6th before Christmas

Moses said to God, 'If I come to the Israelites and tell them that the God of their forefathers has sent me to them, and they ask me his name, what am I to say to them?' God answered, 'I AM that I am. Tell them that I AM has sent you to them.

Exodus 3.13,14 REB

God is other!
Not to be pinned down;
not to be cosily dissected
on a chat show
or through an
in-depth interview
in a Sunday paper.
We can turn human celebrities
inside out,
but not God.

I AM WHAT I AM,
I WILL BE WHAT I WILL BE.

We can
tabulate
and catalogue
minerals,
plants
or animals,
but we cannot
fit God into our neat
little systems,
or tailor the Deity
to our creeds,
structures
and patterns of worship.

I AM WHAT I AM,
I WILL BE WHAT I WILL BE.

We devalue language,
debase and tear to pieces
the very words
which might lead us
to the inner meaning of life:
so we must look beyond words,
beyond language –
and listen
for the silence
in which
the one who has no name
that can be uttered;

Beyond Language

the one we cannot possess
yet who possesses us;
may speak
in the depths
of the seeking heart.

**Help us, we pray,
to put aside agitation,
anxiety,
the quest for instant solutions
to our problems,
and immediate answers
to our questions.**

**Help us to be still –
content that you know us
and that you know
our needs
far better than we do ourselves.**

**Help us to be still –
listening,
yet not worried
if no word is spoken.**

**Help us to be still –
content that in the silence
you are near
and that,
as you have ever done,
you hold us secure
in your love.**

Not A God Of The Gaps

**6th
before
Christmas**

*I shall set my laws in their understanding and write them on their hearts; I
shall be their God, and they will be my people.*

Hebrews 8.10 REB

We thank you,
our heavenly Father,
that though you are a God
greater than our minds can comprehend,
you are not a God of the gaps,
not a God of things
beyond our reach and understanding,
but a God who is with us
in life as we actually have to live it.

You know us through and through,
yet in spite of all the wrong we do,
all the times we turn our backs on your ways,
you still care for us.
Your love reaches out to us
with comfort, forgiveness,
with hope and with strength.

You show us the way of life;
keep us in that way
and defend us from all temptations
to stray from it.
Make us day by day more aware
of your purposes for us
and help us to show
something of your glory in our living.

The Difficulty of Living by Faith

'I am the Alpha and the Omega,' says the Lord God, who is, who was, and who is to come, the sovereign Lord of all.

Revelation 1.8 REB

I believe; help my unbelief.

Mark 9.24b REB

Because I acted in the ignorance of unbelief I was dealt with mercifully;
1 Timothy 1.13 REB

When that day comes, you will not ask me for anything.
John 16.23 GNB

God honours simple faith,
but simple faith is not so easily attained.
It does not come
through shutting tight the minds
God's given us to use;
nor does it arise
out of the arrogant ignorance
that assumes its limited perspective
is the only perspective;
assumes that it can ignore all searching questions
because it trusts in God.

Simple faith is the faith
that God will always be true to himself;
that God will always be
loving,
healing,
rescuing,
however much events
may appear to deny it.
It is the faith that with God
one need be anxious for nothing.

Small wonder
some only come to simple faith
after long struggle,
after being buffeted
by raging storms.

'When that day comes,' said Jesus
'you will not ask me for anything.'

When that day comes,
we will have reached
the perfect simple faith
that knows the Almighty
is to be utterly trusted
through ill and good alike.

How Can We Know?

5th
before
Christmas

Truly I tell you: anything you did for one of my brothers here, however insignificant, you did for me.

Matthew 25.40 REB

It was a good story,
the one about the sheep who were blessed
and the goats who were thrown out;
they liked it
because it confirmed all their prejudices;
they were, of course, the sheep.

The goats were those
who sat lightly to religion
and had no respect
for people who stood for doing things
decently and in order.
It was good to be reminded
that the time would come
when they would get their come-uppance.

But the way Jesus told it
spoiled the story completely.
He dared to suggest
that God had a different perspective,
that you might not be a sheep after all.
Absolute nonsense of course!

**How can we know, Lord,
which people
we are supposed to treat
kindly and considerately?**

**What's that you say?
We can't!**

**Are you telling us
that the only safe way
is to be kind and considerate
to everybody?**

**But everybody Lord?
No exceptions?
You can't really mean that?**

**Surely
Not
EVERYBODY?**

The Promise Of Deliverance

Though the heavens be dispersed as smoke and the earth wear out like a garment and its inhabitants die like flies, my deliverance will be everlasting and my saving power will remain unbroken.

Isaiah 51.6 REB

God of all beginnings and all endings,
we wait for your salvation.
People do die like flies,
and shadows lie over
the whole future of our planet:
and yet –
we have to admit,
it is not the world's disaster zones,
or fears of cosmic catastrophe,
which cast the darkest clouds
over our daily living.

Our own anxieties are more immediate;
health worries,
bills to be paid,
jobs pressing to be done;
the big 'little things'
which threaten
the comfortable cocoons
we spin about ourselves
to create a sense of security.

And so your word of promise
becomes a word of challenge;
for you call us
to look away from ourselves
and our present hopes and fears,
and lift our eyes
to more distant horizons.

**Save us, Lord, from being
so short-sighted, so earthbound,
that we fail to grasp and welcome
the promise of deliverance,
the affirmation
that our ultimate destiny
lies with you, beyond time,
and that all things
past, present and future,
are in your hands,
and yours alone.**

15

Priorities Of The Kingdom
(An Intercession)

The Son of Man will come at the time when you least expect him.
Matthew 24.44 REB

Infinite and Eternal God,
how could we ever begin to know you,
except that you first
made yourself known to us
as a God who breaks into history –
 bringing light to our darkness,
 intervening on behalf of the needy,
 raising up rescuers for the oppressed.

But your coming also reveals
the shoddiness of our service;
men and women cry out to you
for relief from miseries
of which we have little
personal experience,
miseries which we have done
all too little to alleviate.

How can we hear their cry
as you hear it?
Be moved with your compassion?
Feel the wrongs done to your children
as you feel them?

Lord, forgive us that in your Church
we find it so hard
to put first things first;
that we strain at gnats
and swallow camels.
Do not cast us on time's rubbish heap.
Help us to see more clearly your priorities
and to put human need
before careful orthodoxy.
Grant us the will and the strength
to be heralds of your coming,
even though much of that to which we cling
must be destroyed
if the hungry are to be filled
with good things.

Priorities of the Kingdom
(An Intercession)

We pray for those
who cannot receive your good tidings
because they are enslaved
by poverty, sickness or ignorance;
by fear, hatred or bitterness;
for those who are driven
to seek power, prestige
or unnecessary possessions;
and for all who are burdened with guilt.

Quietly we bring to you
the things laid on our own hearts
and lift up those close to us
for whom we would especially
seek your blessing ...

... Yet deal with us
and those for whom we pray
not so much according to our asking
as according to our true needs,
which you alone can know.

We remember those dear to us
who have passed from this world
and we praise you
that through your love
for sinful men and women
they now live in your presence.

God of all things and all people,
may your blessing
rest upon all who seek it.
Give peace in our time, O Lord.
Give peace in our hearts, O Lord.

The Word Beyond The Words

3rd before Christmas (Advent 2)

*So also will be the word that I speak –
it will not fail to do what I plan for it;
it will do everything I send it to do.*

Isaiah 55.11 GNB

We do not have to cling to the Bible as a drowning person might cling to a floating plank. We do not have to hold on for dear life to a few special texts to have all our certainties confirmed. Rather, with humble openness and expectancy, we read the Bible knowing that we are likely to have some of our certainties shattered. We look for new truth and new light. Beyond the printed page we listen for a word spoken in our own hearts, to our own condition and in our own time.

However carefully I read
the Scriptures,
I must listen for the Word
which speaks
beyond the words.

The Word of God
is not embalmed;
nor is it a recorded message –
    'The Almighty regrets
    he is not available at the moment,
    but wishes you to read the prescribed passage
    and follow the instructions you will find there.'
The Word of God
is spoken person to person,
seeking out those who will hear,
and speaking within
the individual heart.

The Word
may grip me
as I quietly read the Scriptures;
or as I join in public worship;
it may wake me in the night;
confront me as I travel;
or leap at me from a news item.
And then I am faced
with a decision;
do I try to pretend
that I have not heard;
do I seek to stifle the Word
with restless activity;
or do I respond?

The Word Beyond The Words

As we read the Scriptures, Lord,
may we do so in humble expectancy,
ready to hear the Word
which speaks to our own situation,
whatever that Word may be.
Help us also, we pray,
to carry that same expectancy
into every part of our daily living,
that we may be able to recognize
your Word when it is spoken to us,
whatever the place
or the occasion,
and however strange
may be the messenger.

First Things First

3rd before Christmas (Advent 2)

You neglect the commandment of God in order to maintain the tradition of men.

Mark 7.8 REB

But surely we need to be
careful about our theology,
mindful of our liturgy;
and scrupulous to do all things
'decently and in order';
how can this be wrong?

What is it, Lord,
that you are saying here?
Are you calling us to think again
about the foundations
of all theology,
all liturgy;
and all conventions and rules;
to look at them again
in the light of
the two commandments
that are one –
'You shall love your God
and you shall love your neighbour
and love them both
with all your heart, soul,
mind and strength'?

> **Lord Jesus,**
> **you have taught us**
> **that love is the fulfilling of the law.**
> **Help us to know better**
> **what love really is –**
> > **how much it may cost**
> > **how far it may lead**
> > **how violently it may threaten**
> > **our ordered way of life –**
> **and then give us the courage**
> **and the generosity of spirit**
> **to accept the way of love**
> **and to walk in it by your Grace**
> **today,**
> **tomorrow**
> **and for the whole**
> **of the rest of our lives.**

Signs Of The Kingdom

Are you the one who is to come, or are we to expect someone else?
Matthew 11.3 REB

Each of the four Gospels tells of the mission of John, preparing through the baptism of repentance for the greater one who should follow. Each tells how Jesus came to be baptized and had at the moment of baptism a special experience of the Holy Spirit. Matthew shows John reluctant to baptize Jesus, declaring that Jesus should really be baptizing him, whilst John has John Baptist testifying of Jesus that he is the Lamb of God who will take away the sin of the world. However, a little later, when he is a prisoner in Herod's fortress, John Baptist is troubled and sends messengers to Jesus asking, 'are you the one who is to come?'.

Why should he doubt? The answer is really quite simple. John Baptist was totally committed to his mission, after all he died for it, but he had his own clear-cut ideas as to what God's Messiah should be like and Jesus didn't fit into them. The weakness of John Baptist was that his preconceived ideas about how God works made it very difficult for him to accept new revelation.

You know how easily, Lord,
we fasten on to a particular way of thinking
and how unwilling we can be
to consider that there might be a larger truth.

Forgive us our closed minds
and the times when we try to fit you
and the Gospel message
into our own preconceptions
and fail to listen
to what you really have to say to us.

Forgive us
our blindness and our deafness,
our lack of love and generosity,
our half-hearted commitment to justice
and our lukewarm striving for peace.

Teach us to discern
the true signs of your kingdom
in changed lives
– often of the most unexpected men and women –
and let the Gospel so work in our hearts
that we may be ready to receive
whatever new revelations
you may have for us.

The Battle with Evil

2nd before Christmas (Advent 3)

He will bring to light what darkness hides and disclose our inward motives.
1 Corinthians 4.5 REB

All that is true ... fill your thoughts with these things.
Philippians 4.8 RE

Source of all truth,
all goodness,
help us, we pray,
in the battle against evil,
especially the evil
which infects our own hearts.

Save us from pride
and all forms of self-deception.
Save us from undue self-concern
and from indifference
to the needs of others.
Save us from the blindness
which sees no difference
between good and evil
and from the sloth
which allows evil
to pass for good.

Strengthen our desire
and our will
to seek out
and to follow
all that is noble,
just, pure, lovely
and gracious.

Guide us, we pray,
into the way
that leads to true happiness
and to the serenity
which comes from living close to you.

Dream And Reality

1st before Christmas (Advent 4)

He has chosen things without rank or standing in the world, mere nothings, to overthrow the existing order.

1 Corinthians 1.28 REB

'Real life' suggests
abrasive human relationships
and a harsh environment.
By contrast, the Christmas story
belongs to the world of dreams.
Yet, in the 'real world',
Herod, dreaming of a dynasty,
slew his own heirs;
and Israel's priests,
dreaming of a God-centred state,
rejected the Messiah.

But whichever we call dream,
whichever we call reality,
life has to be lived
in tension between the two.
We live in the harsh world
of the tabloid headlines
and hold to the glorious truth
of the incarnation – God with us!

It isn't soft lights and carols
or struggle and sadness,
but both!
Not pain and suffering
or joy and deliverance,
but both!
Not heavenly dreams
or earthly reality,
but both!

There is no situation,
however grim,
which may not be touched
and transformed
by the dream, the hope, the reality
which is Christ.
Light has come into the world
and the darkness
will never be able to put it out.

23

Dream And Reality

God of things eternal,
and God of things transitory,
you alone give meaning to our lives.
Help us to be so aware of your presence
that we may trust you
both for what we see
and for what is hidden from us.
Give us the strength we need
to face each new situation as it comes,
and so guide and guard us
that we may faithfully serve you
in our earthly life
and, at its end,
pass through the gates of death
into the life eternal.

Do We Want To Be Saved?

He will save his people from their sins.

Matthew 1.21 REB

Come, Lord Jesus, come!
Come and save us
from the wickedness of this world.
Save us from the evil committed
through pride, greed, lust ...
save us from strife and violence
and from the terrible things
people do to the environment ...

What's that you say, Lord, –
our OWN sins?

But, Lord,
when you think of some of the things
that go on in the world,
it's hardly fair to call our little peccadilloes sins;
they are more idiosyncrasies,
a part of the way we are.
We can't peel them off
as we do our clothes,
it would take something
more like a surgical operation –

Come, Lord Jesus, come, yet –
we hope your coming
won't be too upsetting
We're not sure that we're really ready
for an upheaval in our lives,
especially not at the moment –
not just at Christmas!

> **When we think that we see –
> and we see not;
>   Lord, give us sight.
> When we think that we hear –
> and we hear not;
>   Lord, give us hearing.
> When we think that we live –
> and are dead;
>   Lord, give us life.
> For only with you and in you
> can we ever find our true selves.**

Just An Ordinary Man

Christmas

Do not be afraid to take Mary home with you to be your wife.
Matthew 1.20 REB

He stands in the background
of innumerable nativity scenes
a decent, God-fearing carpenter,
sufficiently established in his trade
to marry and start a family –
only it hadn't worked out
quite as he'd intended!

When he learned
his bride-to-be was pregnant,
and knowing he wasn't the father,
he decided to call the marriage off,
but quietly,
he didn't wish
to make things worse for Mary
than they already were.
Then –
there came the dream!

Joseph accepted the revelation
and took Mary to be his wife.
But were there ever moments
in the years that followed
when he rather ruefully wondered
why he couldn't have been
just an ordinary carpenter,
with an ordinary wife
and an ordinary family?

Father, we thank you
for the faith of those
who, like Joseph,
remain in the background,
but willingly give
strong, caring
and often costly
support to others.
Praise be to you for all
quiet, unobtrusive
servants of the Gospel.

Where Least Expected

Today there has been born to you in the city of David a deliverer.
Luke 2.11 REB

There is strong evidence that Jesus was born in Bethlehem and brought up in Nazareth; but as to the precise date and whether shepherds and wise men actually came, we just cannot know. Yet whether it happened in quite this way or not is relatively unimportant, the story contains truths which still challenge our world; truths which point to a different way of looking at things, a different set of values, a different kingdom.

'The city of David',
but Bethlehem had known better days;
it was now a squalid place
to site a great event;
as though the angel,
coming to us,
should say;
'To find God's sign of hope,
go to Brixton
and look for a baby
in a house for unmarried mothers.'

It is still difficult to accept
that God is to be found in the ordinary
rather than the extraordinary
and on the margins
rather than at the centre.

Insurance policies may exclude
'Acts of God',
meaning all the things
the insurers hadn't already excluded
which could give them a nasty shock;
but if we are to make any sense
of this story of the birth of Jesus,
then 'Acts of God'
are part of the very stuff of life
and they can't possibly
be excluded from anything;
even though
they won't always be recognized
for what they are.

Where Least Expected

Be with us, heavenly Father,
as we keep this festival with fun and gaiety
and the giving and receiving of gifts.
Help us to overcome our selfishness
and our blindness lest,
even as we rejoice,
we turn the holy child from our door.
Strengthen our love and our faith,
that with the wise men
we may see his star,
and with the shepherds
hear the message of the angel.

His Glory?

Christmas

He made his home among us, and we saw his glory ...

John 1.14 REB

The people crowded into Bethlehem that night long ago knew that it was in the Temple or the synagogue that you sought God; they wouldn't have thought of looking for the Almighty in a stable. Yet in the primitive, crude world of the stable a peasant child was born and in him God lived among us. From the day of his birth to the day of his death, Jesus was vulnerable, accessible, giving himself without holding anything back. And this is how his glory was revealed.

God is light –
light which penetrates
the darkness of evil
and can never be totally obliterated.

God is peace –
a sanctuary
amid all the discord, turmoil
and conflicts of life.

God is hope –
and even the clouds of hopelessness
which sometimes engulf us
cannot stifle that hope completely.

God is comfort –
thawing the chill of our deepest sorrows
with warm compassion.

God is healing –
even for the self-inflicted wounds
of our wilful sinfulness.

God is love –
ever reaching out to us;
ever painfully breaking through
the thorny hedges
of the false hopes and dreams
with which we so easily surround ourselves.

God is life –
holding us secure
at the very gates of death,
and beyond.

His Glory?

Yes,
and God is need –
asking of us
gifts we didn't even know we possessed
and enabling us to grow
in the process of giving.

The God who came in Christ
still comes,
still lives among us,
and we still may see his glory.

If we are to live creatively, Lord,
amid the tensions which arise
from our dual citizenship
of earth and heaven,
we shall continually need your help.
Show us how to discharge
our earthly duties
lovingly and responsibly,
but help us also
as we live our daily lives,
to discern the signs of your glory
round about us.

Light the Beacon

Break into songs of triumph ... for the Lord has comforted his people ...
Isaiah 49.13 REB

Light the beacon
Fire the cannon
Sound the trumpet
Tell of a birth
God is present with his people
God is living in his earth.

So sing for joy and sing for love
And sing for truth and sing for right
And take a torch and lift it high
And let the whole world blaze with light.

Strike the drumskin
Rock the belfry
Wake the sleeping
Tell of a birth
God is present with his people
God is living in his earth.

So sing for life and sing for hope
And sing for peace and sing for might
And take a torch and lift it high
And let the whole world blaze with light.

Flash the signal
Beam the message
Launch the rocket
Tell of a birth
God is present with his people
God is living in his earth.

Then jump for joy and leap for love
And dance for truth and skip for right
And take a torch and lift it high
And let the whole world blaze with light.

From *George*

Waiting To Be Recognized
(An Intercession)

On him the spirit of the Lord will rest ...

Isaiah 11.2 RE

To meet us just where we are, Lord,
you came into this world
as a helpless infant.
Help us to see and respond to you
wherever there is an infant
needing love or protection.

As a child you first came to know
your heavenly Father
through the life of your earthly home.
So guide us, that we may
lead the children dear to us
in the ways of your kingdom.

In your earthly ministry
you identified yourself with the poor,
the sick, the sad
and with society's failures and outcasts.
Nourish the seeds of compassion
in our own hearts
that we may seek and serve you
in caring for the deepest needs of others.

We acknowledge you Prince of Peace,
yet our world is full of strife.
We pray for your peace,
starting with peace in our own inner life.
Lord, teach us to seek after
the things that belong to peace,
peace not only for us,
but for all peoples
the world over.

You are the source
of all love and joy
and of all true hope;
yet you also experienced all our sorrows.

Waiting To Be Recognized
(An Intercession)

We pray for those sick, lonely,
sad, or sorrowing at this time.
May they know through their darkness
the light
that no evil
has ever been able totally to extinguish.

We thank you
for every lovely memory
of those dear to us who have died.
We praise you
that they are not lost to us
but have entered into
a new dimension of living
where in your mercy
we believe we shall meet again

You are the Lord who shares our living.
You go with us in all our ways
even when we are blind to your presence
and deaf to your call.
Continue with us we pray,
but make us more aware.
Be born afresh in us.
Renew our lives,
that we may be true witnesses
to the light
offered to every one
who comes into the world.

Song Of Wisdom

Epiphany

King Herod ... called together the chief priests and scribes ... and asked them ...

Matthew 2.4 REB

The wise men thought it ludicrous
To see a group of travellers
Coming from the east
And asking for a king;
They thought they knew the answers,
Though they couldn't feed the starving,
They had nothing for the poorest,
Not those wise, wise men.

    Not the priests or the scribes,
    Not the statesmen or the bureaucrats,
    The judges or the advocates,
    The wisest in the state;
    Not the MPs or the PhDs,
    The ad-men or financiers,
    The pollsters or professors,
    No, nor any of the great.

In the nowhere that was Bethlehem
The travellers found a baby
And they opened up the treasures
They had carried for a king;
They saw hope for the hopeless,
And rescue for the needy,
Truths that weren't apparent
To the wise, wise men.

    Not the television pundits,
    The investigative journalists,
    The media controllers,
    The powers behind the state;
    Not the multi-national managers,
    The dealers in commodities,
    The scientific technocrats,
    No, nor any of the great.

So the question to consider is,
Who really are the wise ones,
Is it those who steal the headlines
Or the ones who seek a king?
It was travellers who found him,
With the will to ask the questions,
With the will to keep on searching,
Not the wise, wise men.

Prayers for Wisdom

Epiphany

And may God, who is the ground of hope, fill you with all joy and peace as you lead the life of faith ...

Romans 15.13 REB

... through the church, the wisdom of God in its infinite variety might be made known ...

Ephesians 3.10 REB

So who among the men and women in this world today are the wise, wise in the biblical sense? Surely it is those who know that life has more to offer than appears on the surface: who seek answers to the deep questions of life which will make sense, not only for them, but for all people: who will follow whatever clue is given to them, wherever it may lead, and who are ready to recognize God meeting them in the simplest needs of the ordinary man, woman or child.

We marvel
that men and women
in Judaea and Galilee
were so blind
when all the time
you were living among them
– and then fear grips us –
what if we have turned our backs on you
or shut the door in your face?
Lord, save us.
Save us from failing to recognize you
when you stand at our side.

**To astrologers searching the night skies
you gave a star.
To shepherds on the whispering hills
you gave a voice.
To fishermen working on the shore
you gave greater work to be done.
What is your sign for me, Lord?
Let me not be blind,
or deaf,
or resistant
when you come.**

A Voice In The Wilderness

1st after Epiphany

There is one coming who is mightier than I ...

Luke 3.16 REI

For it is by grace you are saved through faith ...

Ephesians 2.8 R

From the wilderness,
with his call for repentance
came John,
the baptizer.

And from that other wilderness
of broken relationships
and broken promises;
of cheating
and double-dealing;
of harboured bitterness,
hatred
and malice,
crowds flocked to him,
hoping to make a new beginning.

'I am a voice,' he cried,
'merely a voice.
I am the trailer
for the great event
which is to follow.
Prepare yourselves!
Face up to the evil
in your lives
and change your ways,
God's rescuer is coming.
Prepare the way of the Lord!'

**Stir up in us, Lord,
that sense of urgency
which not only seeks forgiveness
for past follies,
but commits
minds and hearts
to becoming new people;
ready to be used by you
in whatever way you will.**

God Has No Favourites

I now understand how true it is that God has no favourites ...
Acts 10.34 REB

If I may say
to you as God,
I really think
it's rather odd
that in our church
I do not know
a half of those
who also go
and join in Sunday worship.

It also seems
a little queer
that in the church
(if you are near)
that women are,
(since all are one)
not quite the thing,
(at least to some)
to lead the family's worship.

And then the breaking
of the bread,
(if all are one
and Christ is head)
far from uniting us together
provides distinctly
stormy weather
when seeking common worship.

if humankind
is meant to be
before you as
one family,
should we not
in your church begin
to make the
fellowship within
somewhat less

If we're to be
like bees in hive
not Labour
nor Conservative;
and in the world,
not East or West,
if such a wholeness
is the best –

schizo-

phrenic?

The First Thing He Did

2nd after Epiphany

The first thing he did was to find his brother Simon and say to him, 'We have found the Messiah'.

John 1.41 REB

It was Simon who,
with all his faults,
was the natural leader;
but would Simon
ever have been there to lead
if Andrew, the quiet one,
Andrew, the one so ready
to sink back into the shadows,
had not made
seeking out his brother
his top priority?

**Because you found us, Lord,
because we can share with you
joys and sorrows,
fears and hopes;
because we can share
every part of our living,
our days have become that much the richer.
You are both the focus
and the inspiration of our lives.**

**Remind us,
when we need reminding,
that this richness
is not for us alone.**

**Remind us
of our obligation
to share what we have found
with our sisters and brothers
whenever
and wherever
we have opportunity.**

Prevented By The Holy Spirit

2nd after Epiphany

The Holy Spirit did not let them preach the message ...

Acts 16.6 GNB

Door after door
had been shut in their faces,
move after move frustrated,
until at last they reached the coast;
journey's end
and nothing accomplished.

Surely the devil had been at work,
unless ...
unless it was God's way of saying
there was a different enterprise
waiting,
something which so far
hadn't even entered their thoughts.

Then came the dream –
a man of Macedonia!
Paul woke
and acted.
Arrangements quickly made
they set sail
and thus –
the Gospel entered Europe!

> **Teach us, Lord,**
> **to recognize**
> **that you are dealing with us**
> **when doors shut,**
> **just as much as when doors open.**
> **Help us to learn**
> **from difficulties and frustrations**
> **and show us**
> **how to turn them to good account,**
> **how to transform**
> **obstacles into stepping stones.**
> **And if we do go through**
> **a time of fruitless endeavour,**
> **enable us to recognize the moment**
> **when we can again say,**
> **this, Lord,**
> **I can DO!**

Choices

3rd after Epiphany

Today I offer you the choice of life and good, or death and evil.

Deuteronomy 30.15 REB

For me,
it's seldom as simple as that.
Choices are blurred,
one thing has to be weighed
with another,
all too often
there is no obvious
clear-cut good,
but only the choice
between varying degrees
of evil.
Not black or white,
but only indeterminate
shades of grey.

**This I pray, my Lord,
to you, who know my weaknesses.
When I am confused,
the way ahead is far from clear
and I must make difficult choices;
though I may not see
the distant goal,
grant me
guidance for each next step
as it must be taken,
that I stray not over-far
from the path to life.**

The Coming Of Light

3rd after Epiphany

The people that walked in darkness have seen a great light;

Isaiah 9.2 REB

Until the light came,
I did not realize
that I had become so accustomed
to existing in darkness.

Until the light came,
I did not realize
how much rubbish
I had accumulated about me.

Until the light came,
I did not realize
how small the dwelling
in which I had confined myself.

At first it was dazzling, penetrating.
It wasn't easy to adjust to the light.
Too many things stood revealed
I'd rather not have seen.
Yet gradually,
and with fresh and startling clarity,
new hopes, new joys, new life
stood revealed,
waiting for me to grasp them –
if I would!

But I did not have to face
such decisions –
until the light came.

> **Source of light**
> **and source of truth,**
> **do not allow me**
> **to shut out the light**
> **which flows from you.**
> **Enable me to face the truth**
> **about myself**
> **which that light reveals**
> **and strengthen my will**
> **to step with confidence**
> **into whatever new ways**
> **may open before me.**

41

Jacob's Ladder

4th after Epiphany

In a dream he saw a ladder, which rested on the ground with its top reaching to heaven ...

Genesis 28.12 REB

He was sleeping rough,
but at least he was free:
– free of his macho brother;
– free of his senile father;
– free of his mother's cloying love;
– and free of the family's old-time religion.

He'd left them all behind
and a whole new,
adventurous future lay ahead
so, sweet dreams!
Jacob makes himself comfortable
and he sleeps.

> What is that he sees –
> a ladder reaching up to the heavens,
> with angels ascending
> to tell his father's God
> that he is here.
> It's a nightmare!
> The God he thought he'd left behind
> has caught up with him already!

Dawn breaks
on a very different Jacob.
This God he had feared
and hoped to escape;
this God who knows him
all too well;
this very same God
has promised to go with him,
not to harass,
but to bless!

And Jacob the trickster,
Jacob the supplanter,
Jacob the fugitive,
takes a new look
at his own worth
in the sight of God
and responds
to the Almighty's initiative
with open heart,
and with open purse. *(Genesis 28.22b)*

God In All

Everything in heaven and on earth is yours.

1 Chronicles 29.11 REB

Ever-present God,
living as we do
in a world of constant change,
we thank you for every intimation
of things eternal.

> We thank you for those experiences,
> through music, literature, drama, art;
> and through the beauty of the world about us,
> which give us hints
> of greater wonders
> yet to be experienced.

We thank you for all those moments
when our lives
have been touched by loving kindness;
when some of that love
which flows from you
has been made real to us
through another human being.

> We thank you for our churches
> and for all who through the ages
> have been your witnesses,
> passing on the faith
> which we have now inherited.
> We thank you for the knowledge
> that in every continent
> there are Christians
> testifying to the power of the Gospel
> to bring new hope, new life.

Above all, we thank you
for the opportunity
to be counted among your workers
and the promise that,
in losing ourselves in your service
we may truly find fullness of life.

> Glory be to you, our God,
> Father, Son and Holy Spirit
> for your unfailing love
> surrounding us all our days.

43

Here Am I

5th after Epiphany

Here am I! Send me.

Isaiah 6.9 REB

'In the year that King Uzziah died, I saw the Lord.' Uzziah had reigned for fif glorious years. Never since the time of Solomon had national prestige stood s high, but in arrogant pride the King had overstepped himself in the Temple. A the priests sought to restrain him he grew livid with anger and in that moment th white spots of leprosy stood out on his forehead for all to see. Hurried from th temple, triumph turned to disaster, he died not long after, an outcast.

All he had ever accepted,
all he had ever believed
now stood challenged,
discredited.
No firm ground
remained
beneath his feet.
With Uzziah's downfall
the world of the young Isaiah
was shattered,
never to be restored.

Time passed.
Once again he stood
in the Temple,
and this time
he saw the Lord!

In that moment he saw
the emptiness of the success
he had admired and emulated.
As never before
he recognized the evils
of the society in which he lived
and his own
involvement in them.

Confessing his share
in the nation's corporate guilt,
he became aware of the Lord
saying:
'Whom shall I send?'
And Isaiah, hearing
replied,
'Here am I, send me!'

Here Am I

If our hope and trust
have been misdirected.
If we have
all unwittingly
followed after idols;
open our eyes, Lord,
redirect us
to the reality
which does not fail.
Show us the way
you would have us take
and give us the will
and the strength
to respond,
'Here am I!
Send me'.

New Wine, Fresh Skins!

5th after Epiphany

New wine goes into fresh skins!

Luke 5.38 REB

Packaging is the name of the game
and presentation is all-important.
A new carton
to boost sales,
though the product doesn't change.
A new bottle
to stimulate the market,
though there is little difference
in the wine.

But the need
for these particular new wine skins
had nothing to do with marketing.
New skins were essential;
old skins
would be unable to contain
the thrusting force
of the new wine
of the Gospel.

Today,
a lick of paint
on the church noticeboard;
some fresh hymns,
maybe a guitar,
even coffee after the service;
but behind the façade
has anything really changed?
We mustn't forget the skins,
but,
where is the new wine?

We pray for renewal.
Make us ready and willing, Lord,
to update the ways
in which we organize our affairs
and express our faith;
but above all else
renew US!
Renew us from within
and let the new wine of the Gospel
flow through us to the world.

Fast-closed Minds

6th after Epiphany

But they totally failed to understand ...

Luke 6.11 REB

Highly-respected religious leaders,
eager to uphold the laws of God;
their intentions were impeccable,
but their vision was fatally flawed.

The regulations they cherished
were stifling the life
they were seeking to defend;
yet still they shut their minds
against fundamental questions
which might cut from under their feet
the ground on which they stood.

The Law to be overridden
by human need?
Regulations to be broken
merely because there is someone
in distress?
If you once start
down that road
where will you finish?
Better silence
those awkward questions
before it is too late.

It isn't easy, Lord,
to live in the way
of not knowing,
of not being sure.
It's much, much easier
to live by rule
than it is to live by faith.
Yet deep within,
we know your way
is the way we should go.

Lord, we do believe,
vanquish our unbelief.

Part Of A World In Rebellion
(An Intercession)

Cease to do evil, learn to do good.

Isaiah 1.16-17 REB

We come to you, Lord,
knowing we are part of a world
in rebellion against your ways;
a world where we can only serve you
if we are constantly renewed by your Grace.

Teach us, we pray,
what it really means to love,
that we may truly live as your children should.

We pray for the Church where, all too often,
we have made the worship
offered by our sisters and brothers
a cause for hostility and division.
Bind us closer together.
Teach us to value the richness
of our diversity and to rejoice
in every fresh glimpse of your glory
seen through traditions other than our own.

We pray for those separated by arbitrary borders,
ideology or religion.
We pray for those in situations where extremes
of wealth and poverty are bitterly divisive.
We pray for those in situations where
power is grossly abused
and the dispossessed bear the heaviest burdens.

We pray for all who have been nourished
on bitterness and fed with the wrongs
suffered by earlier generations.
We pray for all who have grown to hate people
instead of hating that which evil does to people.
We pray for those who are impatient for change
and for those who resist all change.

Despite all the times we fail you, Lord,
we would heal, and not destroy;
teach us the discipline of obedience to the commandment
'You shall love your neighbour as yourself',
and give us the will and the fortitude
to go on obeying that command to the end.

48

Consider The Sower

Listen! A sower went out to sow.

Mark 4.3 REB

Long before the days of mechanization, a farmer goes out to sow his field. As he walks up and down, he sows handful by handful, steadily, methodically. He knows from the start that some of the seed must be wasted; that a path will be trodden across his land, that there are hidden rocks, weeds he hasn't been able to eradicate and that the birds are sure to be busy. These are facts of the only life he knows, but they don't lead him to say 'It isn't worth it, I'm going to give up farming'. He gets on with the job, and despite all frustrations and disappointments he reaps a harvest. And that, said Jesus, is what it is like working for the kingdom of God.

We too, Lord, would learn from the sower.
Help us to do faithfully
whatever work is put into our hands.
Help us to accept that there will be
frustrations and disappointments,
that some of our efforts
are sure to be wasted
and that there will be days
when we feel so low
that we are tempted to give up altogether.
When such times come,
turn our thoughts, we pray,
to the difficulties with which you contended,
the sorrows and disappointments you faced
and the pain you bore,
that we,
with men and women the world over,
might come to know
life in all its fullness.

49

The Search For Truth

9th before Easter

If you cry out for discernment and invoke understanding, if you seek for her as for silver and dig for her as for buried treasure, then you will understand the fear of the Lord and attain to knowledge of God.

Proverbs 2.3-5 REB

The search for truth,
the asking of questions concerning
    – the nature of the universe,
    – the unimaginable vastness of space,
    – the equally unimaginable complexity
        of matter which the eye cannot see,
    – the origins of life,
        and what it is to be human
does not take us further from God.

It may destroy
false and inadequate images of God
which clutter our minds;
but it can only bring us closer
to the one who is the source of all truth
and in whom all things
live and move and have their being.

God, all in all,
giver and renewer of life,
we worship and adore you.
Lord Jesus Christ,
through whom alone
we know the love
which is at the heart of God,
we worship and adore you.
Holy Spirit of God,
source of all light and truth,
we worship and adore you.

'Not One Of Us'

**8th
before
Easter**

A Canaanite woman from those parts came to meet him ...
Matthew 15.22 REB

Missing from this story
is the 'body language'.
The words are harsh,
but what we cannot see
is the look in Jesus' eye,
the hint maybe of a smile,
or the gesture,
which encouraged the woman to persist.

If the disciples had had their way,
she would have been sent packing;
she was certainly 'not one of us'.
Jesus heard them,
and as he probed
the woman's response
to the fact that his mission
was firstly to his own people,
he was also educating his companions.

The woman's answer pleased him.
She refused to be discouraged;
she believed he could
and would
heal her daughter,
and, despite the disciples,
he sent her away satisfied.

**Save us, Lord, from trying to set limits
on who may or may not be acceptable to you.
Help us to face up to our prejudices
and to master them;
for you have shown us
that your love
and your healing
are for any and every human soul.**

Unanswered Prayer?

8th before Easter

Three times I begged the Lord to rid me of it ...

2 Corinthians 12.8 REB

He wasn't healed,
although he prayed for healing.
'Three times I begged the Lord',
three periods of anguished prayer
that he might be delivered,
yet Paul's 'thorn in the flesh'
remained to trouble him
with recurring weakness
that led to mocking
and ridicule.

Would God indeed
use such a one
as a 'Chosen instrument'?
We know the answer.
God would,
God did,
God does!

> **When we seek strength to overcome weakness,**
> **beg for release from infirmity,**
> **and our prayer is not answered**
> **in the way we could wish;**
> **then grant, Lord, in your mercy,**
> **that our hearing may be tuned**
> **to receive the word –**
> **'My Grace is all you need;**
> **power is most fully seen in weakness.' –**
> **that even our disability**
> **may become a channel for your Grace.**

In The Eye Of The Storm

We are sinking!

Mark 4.38 REB

They had handled boats
on that sea
since they were boys
and yet they panicked,
forgot their skills
in navigation
and cried out like novices
for rescue.

It was the inner storm
that needed to be stilled.
The fear
that had suddenly
emasculated them.

Jesus took command.
'Peace, be still',
and because they trusted him
the fear left them,
and they were able
to return to
sailing their vessel
once again.

**We also can be
hit by sudden storms
which threaten to overwhelm us.
If we come to such a time of testing
and are in danger of panicking,
let us feel your presence, Lord,
and hear you saying
'Peace, be still',
that we may find renewed confidence
and the strength to sail
the next stage of our voyage,
wherever it may take us.**

Dealing With Us In Mysteries
(An Intercession)

7th before Easter

And my God will supply all your needs out of the magnificence of his riches in Christ Jesus.

Philippians 4.19 REB

From a prison cell, having faced pains, sorrows and hardships ever since his conversion on the road to Damascus, and with a likely sentence of death hanging over him, Paul can still write a letter full of confidence and joy to the Philippian Christians and assert that God will supply all needs.

You deal with us in mysteries, Lord.
You offer us peace,
not as withdrawal from struggle,
but peace in the very heart of struggle.
You offer us joy and happiness,
not as one great perpetual holiday,
but as a call to ever deeper commitment.
You offer us the greatest of all freedoms,
not to go off and do just as we like
and quickly be miserable,
but freedom to lose ourselves
in choosing to follow you.

Continue to deal with us,
not according to our asking,
but according to our needs.
Break through whatever clouds
may obscure you from us,
that we may see more clearly what it is
you would have us make of our living.

We pray for our world;
the everyday world in which we live and work
and meet people in the street or shops:
how can we be your witnesses in this world?

Never let us forget
that we are part of all peoples
on the face of the earth,
but don't let us get so busy
thinking of the needs of those far away
that we forget the needs
of people on our own doorstep.

Dealing With Us In Mysteries
(An Intercession)

There are things that trouble us,
not just concerning ourselves,
but the needs of people we love.
Reassure us that you love them too;
that, however much we think we love them,
your love is greater and enfolds us all.
Save us from getting bogged down with anxieties
and help us to live
fully and freely as your people should.

Rekindle the sense of adventure
and the sheer excitement of your service,
strengthen our trust
where we cannot understand
and keep us in the way of Jesus
this day
and every day of our lives.

Create A Little Space

Ash Wednesday

When you pray, go into a room by yourself, shut the door, and pray to your Father who is in secret.

Matthew 6.6 REB

Create a little space.

Take time for stillness;
put aside for a moment
the many things
waiting to be done.

Create a little space.

Take time for stillness;
picture afresh
the people about you
until you can hold them
in deeper love and understanding.

Create a little space.

Take time to listen.
Always there is the danger
in our activity-filled days
that we shall
hear and fail to hear,
see and fail to see;
be busy, but with wrong priorities.

Create a little space.

Take time for stillness,
time for the mind to lie fallow,
time for renewal,
time for the Spirit.

Create a little space.

A New Creation

Hate evil, and love good.

Amos 5.15 REB

For anyone united to Christ, there is a new creation: the old order has gone; a new order has already begun.

2 Corinthians 5.17 REB

We are poor disciples, Lord.
Save us, we pray,
from dwelling on any hurt to our pride
which could lead to anger.
Save us
from nursing grudges and resentments
and from refusing to love and forgive.
Save us
from the self-centredness
which makes us blind to the needs of others;
and save us
from refusing the time, money or effort
which might be spent creatively in your name.
Enable us to be a part of your new creation
and lead us into the way of life.

> **Show us, Lord Jesus,**
> **how to live**
> **in the way that you lived,**
> **respecting others,**
> **however poor**
> **or unattractive they may be.**
> **Teach us to do simple jobs**
> **as you would do them,**
> **quietly and thoroughly,**
> **not worrying if we are not given**
> **more exciting duties.**
> **Teach us to value**
> **all the gifts you have given us**
> **and to treat them as a trust**
> **to be used in your service.**
> **We do want to be your people,**
> **work upon us, we pray,**
> **that we may increasingly**
> **be aware of your presence,**
> **and grow to live nearer to your ways.**

In Time Of Temptation

**6th
before
Easter**

*No one when tempted should say, 'I am being tempted by God'; for God can-
not be tempted by evil and does not himself tempt anyone.*

James 1.13 REB

Not all bad choices are blameworthy;
decisions must sometimes be made
with inadequate information,
or with all too little time for thought,
and, with the best of intentions,
we can get it wrong!

Temptation implies awareness.
We know the choice we should make
yet feel the seduction of another way.
We may rationalize,
and give ourselves strong reasons
for choosing a different path,
but underneath
the awareness remains
that we have chosen knowingly,
and chosen wrongly.

Thank God that this is so:
if we could totally stifle conscience,
lose all awareness
of the difference between good and evil,
we should come dangerously near
to the death of the soul.

> **Wake me Lord from deathly slumbers,**
> **Save me now and evermore.**
> **Free me from my selfish striving,**
> **Save me now and evermore.**
> **Tame in me unbridled passions,**
> **Save me now and evermore.**
> **Nerve and steel my coward spirit,**
> **Save me now and evermore.**
> **Show me love in all its splendour,**
> **Save me now and evermore.**
> **Father, Son and Holy Spirit**
> **Save me now and evermore,**
> **Save me now and evermore.**

From *Out Of This World*

Make Us Aware

The kingdom of God is upon you. Repent, and believe the gospel.
Mark 1.14 REB

Loving Father,
so often
we go thoughtlessly through life
and miss much
because we are not looking
for the signs of your presence.
We are too ready
to listen uncritically
to the pronouncements of experts
or to trust too much
to our own skills and judgement;
much of the time
we behave as though you didn't exist.
Make us aware, Father,
make us aware!

**Saviour Lord,
we ask your forgiveness
for the times
when we shut our eyes to your glory
and turn our backs on your truth;
for the times
when we refuse to be guided by the Spirit
and wilfully go our own ways.
Rescue us from the darkness
into which we plunge ourselves
and lead us back to the light,
that we may be forgiven,
and our feet set afresh
on the road to the kingdom.**

Divine Madness

5th before Easter

'He is out of his mind', they said.

Mark 3.21 RE

'Madness', they said,
'this is madness',
and his family,
fearful for him
and for themselves
would,
if they could,
have stopped him in his tracks
and taken him back
to the carpenter's bench.

Of course he was mad.
Mad to become a wandering preacher.
Mad to antagonize his neighbours
    in his home synagogue.
Mad to clasp a leper,
    defend an adulteress.
Mad to talk of loving enemies.
Mad to provoke the establishment.
Mad to let himself be taken and crucified.

But in such divine madness
is all our hope.
In such madness
lies the salvation of the world.

**You trouble us, Lord;
you turn all our values
on their head,
you won't leave us alone
until at last
the scales fall from our eyes
and we see
that your ways
are our only hope,
that your madness
is the ultimate sanity.**

The Unseen Host

5th before Easter

The Lord opened the young man's eyes, and he saw the hills covered with horses and chariots of fire all around Elisha.

2 Kings 6.17 REB

Horses and chariots of fire
covered the hills around Elisha,
but they never intervened.
It was Elisha who,
by a stratagem,
drew off the besiegers from the city.
Elisha saw the hosts of heaven,
but they never intervened.

The twelve or more legions of angels
of which Jesus spoke in Gethsemene
never intervened.
Jesus, hanging on the cross,
himself bore the weight
of the follies of humanity.
Jesus was conscious
of the hosts of heaven,
but they never intervened.

To the few is granted
vision to see beyond the finite world,
but even they must still engage
in their own skirmishes
with the enemy.
Though the hosts of heaven
are committed to the fray,
we each must stand our ground
where God has set us,
and complete the work
the Almighty
has put into our hands.

From *Prophets in Action*

The Unseen Host

When it appears that
we are fighting a losing battle,
and we fear that we shall be overwhelmed
by the enemy;
strengthen our faith, Lord,
and remind us again
that not only our little victories,
but even our seeming defeats
may have their place
in the ultimate triumph
of your kingdom.

Who Is This? (Caesarea Philippi)

4th before Easter

Who do you say I am?

Mark 8.29 REB

And still he asks,
'Who do you say I am?'
and some reply –

> You are an idealist,
> a visionary,
> a great religious leader
> like the Buddha or Mahomet,
> worthy of admiration and respect
> but somewhat unrelated
> to these present times.

'And you', he asks,
'Who do you say I am?'.

> What answer do we make?
> Do we, like Peter, say,
> 'You are the Christ,'
> and promptly try to fit the Lord
> into our own preconceived ideas
> of what that means?

> Do we also deserve to hear
> that stern rebuke,
> 'Out of my sight,
> your earthbound expectations
> serve the devil,
> not your God'?

> **When we come to you**
> **and call you Lord,**
> **look for your help**
> **to carry out our plans,**
> **throw everything upon you**
> **except the question**
> **'Which way would you have us go?'**
> **forgive us our foolishness**
> **and help us to become**
> **more willing to listen,**
> **more willing to be redirected;**
> **that we may honour you as Lord**
> **in deed as well as word.**

63

The Ultimate Security

Their Maker will not fail them.

1 Peter 4.19 REB

The life I now live is not my life, but the life which Christ lives in me.
Galatians 2.20 RE

Creator and sustainer of all that is,
we praise you for the gift of life
and for all the wonders of the world
in which you have set us;
but above all we praise you
that you have not left us to our own devices
or cast us off because of our follies.
You are a God
who breaks into life
again and again,
and when you come to us,
you come to help
and to save.

Mighty and loving God,
we rejoice that through the Holy Spirit
you are ever with us;
that we are never left
to face our troubles alone.
We thank you for –
Strength to match our weakness,
Comfort to lighten our distress,
Guidance to lead us in perplexity,
Inner peace to hold us against disaster,
Love to dissolve our bitterness and
Forgiveness to cover our failures.
So much has been given to us,
help us in our turn to be channels
through which your blessing may flow
to others in their times of need.

When Reason Is Not Enough

3rd before Easter

Could not this perfume have been sold ... and the money given to the poor?
John 12.5 REB

Stewards of God's riches,
committed to acting wisely
and using resources prudently;
surely we must deplore
such wasteful extravagance.
So many meals
might have been provided for the hungry,
or blankets,
or warm clothing:
that would have been
the reasonable thing to do.

And yet –
it seems the Lord
would have us learn
that there are times
when reason alone is not enough;
it must be tempered
by the warmth of a loving heart
and love will sometimes overflow
in wild extravagance.
Love lay behind the impulsive gift
and Jesus willingly received it.
'There will be many other opportunities',
he said, 'to serve the poor'.

And in the years that followed,
how many hungry souls,
I wonder,
were fed by Mary
for Jesus' sake?
Many more,
I dare to guess,
than that one flask of oil
could ever have satisfied.

When Reason Is Not Enough

You have given us minds, Lord,
and we must use them
if we are to serve you
to the best of our ability.
But let your spirit so guide us
that we may temper reason with love
and recognize loving acts in others
even if, at times,
they may appear a little unreasonable
to our rational ways of thinking.

Prayers On Mothering Sunday

**3rd
before
Easter**

As a mother comforts her son so shall I myself comfort you ...
Isaiah 66.13 REB

O Jerusalem, Jerusalem ... How often have I longed to gather your children, as
a hen gathers her brood under her wings; but you would not let me.
Matthew 23.37 REB

We give thanks –
For every home where children
    are nurtured in loving care
    and grow to value
    the ways of integrity, service and compassion:
For every family
    where loving ties bind the generations
    and young and old together
    can joyfully give and receive:
For the many-faceted Church,
    which despite both persecution and indifference
    has through the centuries
    offered a fellowship in which
    we may learn from
    and grow closer to our Saviour:
And for the testimony
    that at the heart of our
    mysterious and wonderful universe
    there is a love that would
    gather us to itself.

We pray for all children
who have been denied
a settled family life:
For all, both young and old,
who suffer the pain of broken homes
and fractured human relationships:
For all, but especially the young,
who are homeless:
And we confess with shame
the contradictions and divisions
within the Church which hinder
our witness to the loving parent God
who would visit every family
in every place with blessings.

Prayers On Mothering Sunday

Lord, we pray that we may know ourselves
so secure in your love that in our turn
we may be able to give ourselves in love to others,
building caring relationships
and creating ever-widening family circles
for your sake who care for us all.

While We Were Yet Sinners

2nd before Easter

But Christ died for us while we were yet sinners, and that is God's proof of his love towards us.

Romans 5.8 REB

This world that God loves can be an incredibly beautiful world, but it is also a world that knows the horrors of drought, flood, volcanic eruption, earthquake and the greater horrors that come through human power struggles: lying, cheating, thieving, oppressing, torturing, or through sheer indifference to the needs of those who are weak or hurt.

It is a world that can produce saints and martyrs, but also drug pushers and completely unscrupulous manipulators of money and commodities. Yet we can still believe that God really and truly loves the world because in Jesus of Nazareth he was totally involved in the world and so cared, that he accepted crucifixion for the sake and at the hands of those he loved. He gave and he gives in a loving that is without limit and without end.

One Friday in eternity
A man was framed they say,
A man was framed, but why the fuss,
It happens every day;
With all the trappings of the law
It happens every day.
One Friday in Eternity
Repeated every day.

One Friday in Eternity
A man was flogged they say,
A man was flogged, but why the fuss,
It happens every day;
Imprisoned, brainwashed, tortured, starved,
It happens every day.
One Friday in Eternity
Repeated every day.

One Friday in Eternity
A man was hung they say,
A man was hung, but why the fuss,
It happens every day;
Hung, shot or crucified, who cares,
It happens every day,
One Friday in Eternity
Repeated every day.

While We Were Yet Sinners

One Friday in Eternity
That man was God they say,
If that is true – if God was there –
It happens every day;
If God is sharing mortal pain
It happens every day.
One Friday in Eternity
Repeated every day.

From *One Friday In Eternity*

Father God,
in Jesus we have learned
that there are no limits to your love.
As we marvel at the way
in which you give yourself to us,
may we come to desire you
with our whole heart:
that seeking, we may find you,
and finding, we may love you,
and loving you,
we may hate the sins
from which you have redeemed us
through Jesus Christ our Lord.

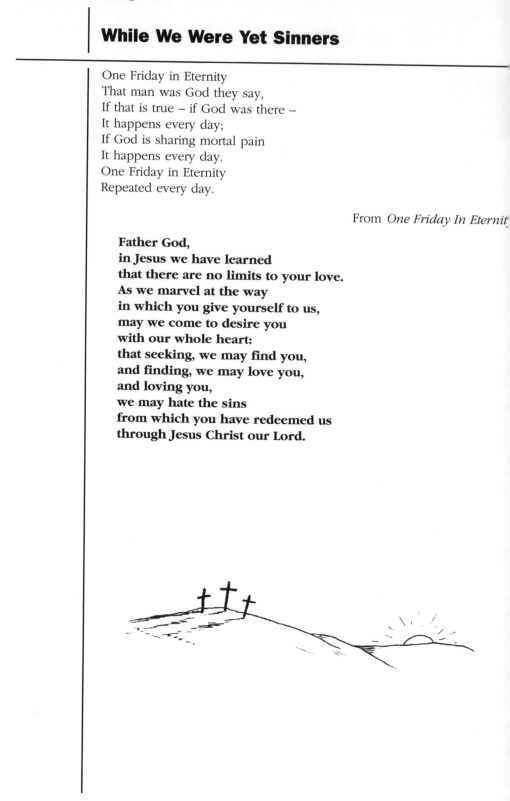

From The Centre To The Margins

2nd before Easter

For the Son of Man did not come to be served but to serve, and to give his life as a ransom for many.

Mark 10.45 REB

Christ was rejected and crucified;
but this was only the climax of a life
where he was poor amongst the poor;
a life where he singled out
for special care
those whom even the poor
despised or feared.

In Christ,
the God who is at the centre of all things
took the centre to the margins,
and that is still
where he is most likely to be found.

It is not when we are confident and strong,
but when we are fragile;
when we are off balance;
when our world has disintegrated,
our self-confidence has vanished,
and our sins rise up to haunt us
– that is when he is closest.

And the word he has for us,
if we will hear it,
whatever that word may be,
will always be a word
spoken out of the immensity of his love.

**If I ever reach the point
of utterly despising myself
and writing off all I have ever done
as useless, or worse;
then, even if I have ceased
to seek for you,
in your mercy, Lord,
continue to seek for me.
Remind me again
that you write off nobody;
that you are still seeking
those who are lost
to rescue them
and bring them home again
to the Father's house.**

71

Your Love Is So Vulnerable

1st before Easter (Palm Sunday)

When he came in sight of the city, he wept over it and said, 'If only you had known this day the way that leads to peace!'

Luke 19.41-42 REB

Father, your love is so vulnerable –
We learn this from Jesus
as he approached the hostile city
and wept over it.
Age after age
you bear the burden
of our follies
and our wilful sins.
You lay yourself open
to our spite and pettiness,
our dishonesty and malice;
you know us through and through
and are constantly being wounded by us,
yet you still care for us,
still love us.
Father, forgive us our insensitivity,
our absorption with ourselves
and all the evil things we do.
Lead us into the way of repentance
and help us to become
more ready to love
in the way that you love,
more worthy to bear
the name of Christian.

The Ways Of The Kingdom

See, your king is coming to you ... humble and mounted on a donkey ...
Zechariah 9.9 REB

So simply,
so unassumingly,
you show us the path to life;
yet we do not find it easy to follow it.
We are glad,
as were your disciples
at your entry into Jerusalem,
glad that you come to us as king;
yet, like those disciples,
we shrink at the cross.
Help us, Lord, to value
and to make our own
the ways of your
so very different kingdom.
Teach us the strength of love
and the power of forgiveness.
Teach us the way of true humility,
that we may be free of all
arrogance and pretension.
Deal with our hesitancy and our fears
and give us strength to follow
where you would lead,
that we may truly come to know
the joy of being citizens
of your kingdom.

**Let love come among us,
let praise be on our lips,
let adoration be in our hearts,
and let gentleness mark
our dealings one with another;
in the name of him who came
seated on a donkey,
and who for our sakes
accepted death on a cross,
Jesus our King.**

The Upper Room

Maundy Thursday

'This is my body, which is for you' ... *'This cup is the new covenant sealed by my blood'* ...

1 Corinthians 11.24-25 REB

When we bless the cup of blessing, is it not a means of sharing in the blood Christ? When we break the bread, is it not a means of sharing in the body Christ? Because there is one loaf, we, though many, are one body; for it is on loaf of which we all partake.

1 Corinthians 10.16-17 RE

Christ died for me!
He died for me personally,
but he did not die for me exclusively.
I cannot celebrate
the death of my Lord
in isolation.
Yes, Christ died for me,
but for me together with
each and every one
of my sisters and my brothers
the whole world over.

Christ invites each and all
to gather at his table,
to become part of his body
and, as part of his body,
part of one another
in loving fellowship.

Yet the mystery and the wonder
of what Christ has done for us
is proclaimed,
not so much at his table
as when we leave that table
and return to the everyday world.

Christ is acknowledged
or rejected
by the way in which we behave
towards our fellow Christians,
and towards all other
men and women, near and far:
for like them,
or like them not,
each and all are sisters and brothers
for whom Christ died.

The Upper Room

Crucified and risen Lord,
you know our weaknesses and our prejudices,
the confusions in our thinking,
the short-sighted and selfish aims
which so often shape
the direction of our living.
By your patience with the foolish
and your compassion for the weak;
by your hatred of sin
and your love for sinners;
by your perfect obedience to the Father
and your strong humility;
forgive us our follies.
Deal with the wickedness in our hearts
and bring us closer to yourself,
to the knowledge of the Father
and the fellowship of the Holy Spirit.
These things we ask for the love
which you have for us all.

Total Commitment

Maundy Thursday

Peter said, 'Even if I have to die with you, I will never disown you.' And all the disciples said the same.

Matthew 26.35 REB

'Abba, Father,' he said,
'all things are possible to you;
take this cup from me.'

Ahead lay physical agony,
humiliation,
rejection;
but even worse,
the disciples he had so lovingly
gathered and taught
were not ready
for what was to come;
they still looked for
the wrong sort of kingdom;
still awaited
the wrong sort of miracle.
Was this then the end,
his work lost,
his life given in vain?

'Abba, Father,' he said,
'all things are possible to you;
take this cup from me.
Yet not my will but yours.'

Mark 14.36 REB

**Like your disciples, Lord,
we have protested our loyalty
and then failed you miserably.
You trod the way of love unflinchingly,
we are liable to hesitate at every step.
We fear the pain and the suffering
which love can bring,
yet deep in our hearts
we know that your way
is the only true way to life.
Lord, forgive us what we are
and help us on the way to becoming
what you would have us be.**

Were You There?

Good Friday

Then they fastened him to the cross.

Mark 15.24 REB

A carpenter speaks:

So I nailed him to the cross.
I'm not proud of it,
but I'm not hiding it either;
it was all in the day's work as you might say
and you'd have done the same in my place
because you couldn't do any other.
You have to do your job if you're going to live,
too many questions and you're a liability,
next thing you know, you're redundant.

So I nailed him to the cross.
Alright, so I did;
but what about the bloke who sold him down the river,
and the ones who fixed the evidence,
and the noble judge,
and all those loyal supporters who conveniently disappeared?

So, I nailed him to the cross.
I'd have been glad not to,
after all, he was a carpenter too;
but under orders you'd have done the same.
You disobey a lawful order in a 'national emergency'
and see where it gets you.
So don't go putting the blame on me.
If you want to blame someone,
if you really must blame someone,
why not start with yourself?

From *One Friday In Eternity*

Were You There?

A Veneer of Civilization

The evil which we see at the cross is the familiar evil in your heart and in mine. Paul was quite right, sin is not just what other people do. Christ died for *our* sins. The twist, the bias, runs through all humankind.

New marvels about the nature of the universe continue to be revealed. Human beings have shown themselves capable of amazing technical achievements and the electronics revolution continues. But when the mask is off, are we more humane? More honest? Less self-seeking? More compassionate? Are we, beneath the skin, really any different from those of whom we read, 'They crucified him there'?

I can't answer for you, only for myself. There is a veneer of civilization on me yet I fear that, like the veneer on furniture which has been badly treated and exposed to damp, it will all too easily curl and peel and chip. I know that I haven't outgrown the need for a Saviour to rescue me from myself.

> **We are ordinary men and women, Lord,**
> **we don't do half the good we might do**
> **and there are times**
> **when we do foolish and evil things;**
> **the worst of it is**
> **that often we don't even realize**
> **how foolish and evil they are.**
> **Help us to know ourselves better,**
> **however painful that knowledge may be.**
> **Forgive us the evil we do**
> **and the pain we cause you;**
> **strengthen what is good in us,**
> **and guide us in the days ahead**
> **that we may become**
> **more able**
> **and more willing**
> **to follow where you would lead.**

The Helpless Saviour

Good Friday

'He saved others,' they said, 'but he cannot save himself.'

Mark 15.31 REB

He hangs berated, outcast, scorned,
No angel comes to set him free,
To all the world a spectacle
Transfixed upon that barren tree.

No lightning strikes the mocking crowd,
No voices echo from the skies,
Alone upon that fearful cross
In agonizing pain he dies.

No miracles, no mighty acts,
No halo bright around his head,
Nailed by our bitter enmity
The Saviour of the world is dead.

So many crosses have been raised,
So many crosses yet to come,
Bearing again our human pain
He dies again in every one.

What though he came to be our peace,
He makes no terms with hate or pride;
His living presence is a threat
We dare not face 'til self has died.

From *A Song For Easter*

'He saved others, but he cannot save himself.' Of course he couldn't, that was the whole point. At the heart of all sin, all rebellion against the things of God, is self-interest, and saving love has to be bigger than this. Saving love has to be free of all self-centredness. We who throughout our lives are driven by self-interest of one sort or another, see here the one in whom self-interest had no part. He couldn't save himself because it wasn't in his nature to save himself. All his love, all his power was directed away from himself to others. No, he couldn't save himself – but from our selfish fears, from our petty pride, from our limited horizons, from the mean actions we clothe with high-sounding principles, from all the sins named and nameless that imprison us, he can and he will save you and me.

The Seven Words From The Cross

No one Gospel gives all the 'seven words'. Mark and Matthew each have 'My God, my God, why have you forsaken me'. Luke has, 'Father forgive them', 'Today you will be with me in Paradise', and 'Father, into your hands I commit my spirit'. John has, 'Mother there is your son – there is your mother', 'I am thirsty' and 'It is accomplished'. Following a long tradition, the seven are here brought together in what appears the most likely order.

The Seven Words From The Cross (1)

Good Friday

Father forgive them; they do not know what they are doing.

Luke 23.34 REB

Who were the ones who didn't know?
    Soldiers – obeying orders:
    religious leaders – upholding the faith:
    civil authorities – keeping the peace:
    the crowd – eager for the latest spectacle
    yes, and sympathizers – busy keeping their heads down.
And Jesus cried,
'Father forgive them;
they do not know what they are doing'.

'Were you there when they crucified my Lord?'
Yes Lord,
we were there;
we *are* there.
All of us are there
and the tragedy is
that it takes a crucifixion
to make us aware of the fact.

> **Father, forgive us the sins**
> **which at the time**
> **don't seem all that terrible;**
> **but are sins which play a part**
> **in crucifying others.**
> **Forgive us**
> **our hasty judgements,**
> **our hiding behind custom or tradition**
> **and our refusals**
> **to face upsetting criticisms.**
> **Forgive us**
> **our unwillingness to be involved**
> **in other people's troubles**
> **and the plausible excuses**
> **with which we deny responsibility,**
> **or assume we have discharged it**
> **with a small donation to a worthy cause.**
> **And forgive us that we manage**
> **to so dull our senses**
> **that most times**
> **we do not even know what we are doing.**
> **Father forgive,**
> **Forgive ...**

81

The Seven Words From The Cross (2)

Good Friday

Truly I tell you: today you will be with me in Paradise.

Luke 23.43 REB

'Jesus, remember me
when you come to your throne.'
That was all he said.

He didn't say,
'I believe you are the Christ'.
He didn't even say,
'Jesus, forgive';
just,
'Jesus, remember me;
remember the robber
who found himself
so unwillingly at your side'.

He received no instruction,
he made no profession of faith,
he was never baptized!

Is the love of God in Christ
so comprehensive?
If this was enough for a robber
to enter Paradise,
what happens to
ecclesiastical protocol?

**Jesus, your love has a way
of breaking through barriers
and reaching out
in unexpected ways
to unexpected people.
It is a love
so much greater than our own
and we suspect
that it includes people
whom we have written off.
Forgive us our failures of love
and in your mercy
bring us at the end
to be together
with all your people
in the eternal kingdom.**

The Seven Words From The Cross (3)

Good Friday

Mother, there is your son ... there is your mother.

John 19.26-27 REB

Through excruciating pain
Jesus could reach out
to the needs of his mother
and his dear disciple, John.
Nailed to the cross
and seemingly helpless,
he not only felt their anguish,
but offered healing
for the bitter grief
which now engulfed them.

The love that held them
rooted to the spot,
watching him die
must be rechannelled.
Though it was agony to speak,
he found the words
to commit each
to the other;
that was how
their love for him
must be expressed
in the days that lay ahead.

**When a loved one
is torn from us
and we grieve
and are desolate;
point us, Lord,
to others who need our love,
that in giving
we may again
be able to receive.**

The Seven Words From The Cross (4)

Good Friday

Eloï, Eloï, lema sabachthani? ... My God, my God, why have you forsaken me?
Matthew 27.46, Mark 15.34 REB

That awful, spine-chilling cry!
Helpless and racked with pain,
even Christ felt
utterly alone,
forsaken,
abandoned.

Reaching rock bottom,
can anything be worse
than feeling God is
blind,
deaf,
heartless,
or dead?

Yet
'God was in Christ',
and Christ's agony
in that specific moment of time
has become timeless;
become part of the very being of God.

'God was in Christ',
and so God knows
what it is to despair
and bids us trust
and go on trusting;
bids us hold on
and keep holding on,
though it be
only by our fingertips.

Help us, Father,
when things are at their worst,
to hold on to the truth
that in Christ
you are in the situation with us.
Whisper to us again
that firm ground lies beyond the quagmire;
light beyond the darkness;
and rejoicing beyond the despair.

84

The Seven Words From The Cross (5)

I am thirsty.

John 19.28 REB

Even Jesus thirsted!

Hanging on the cross,
even Jesus
needed
someone willing to moisten
his parched lips.

To us Jesus
is bread
and water of life,
nourishing us
for the life eternal.
Yet he knew
the pressing needs
of the human body;
he hungered in the wilderness;
he thirsted on the cross.

And still he thirsts.
Where men and women
suffer hunger;
where children
die for lack
of clean water,
the cry from the cross
is again heard
'I am thirsty'.

**Do not allow us to forget, Lord,
that in the needs
of the hungry
and the thirsty
it is you who are asking
for our aid.
Save us, we pray,
from failing you,
by failing them.**

The Seven Words From The Cross (6)

It is accomplished!

John 19.30 REI

But what was accomplished?
Here we are confronted
with the deepest of mysteries;
a crucified man,
helpless,
derided,
racked with pain,
cries out
as one in control
of his destiny,
'It is accomplished'.

This cry defies all worldly wisdom,
it questions all worldly power;
the human intellect
cannot cope
with such foolishness.
Only the heart can know
that this was the folly of God
and that what here was accomplished
was the salvation of the world,
and from the heart we cry –

> **Glory to God, in whom**
> **everything that is has its being.**
> **Glory to Jesus, by whom**
> **the loving, rescuing nature of God**
> **has been revealed in a human life.**
> **Glory to the Holy Spirit, through whom**
> **God is at work in our lives today.**
> **To the creating, saving,**
> **ever-present God,**
> **be glory and praise for ever.**

The Seven Words From The Cross (7)

Father, into your hands I commit my spirit.

Luke 23.46 REB

And now
the full humanity of Christ,
with all its joys
and all its pains,
is freely given
and freely received
into the Godhead.

'I go to prepare a place for you', he said, *(John 14.2 AV)*
and to each and every one of us
he offers welcome
to the eternal kingdom.

> **God of all time,**
> **God of all things,**
> **and God of all peoples;**
> **through our Lord Jesus Christ**
> **you have made yourself known to us**
> **as a loving, rescuing God;**
> **defend us from all**
> **that would separate us**
> **from your loving care,**
> **and strengthen our purpose**
> **to serve our Lord**
> **with heart and soul**
> **and mind and strength**
> **all the days of our earthly life;**
> **and of your great mercy**
> **forgive us our many sins**
> **and bring us at the last**
> **to your eternal kingdom.**

The Whisper

Easter Day

Go quickly and tell his disciples: 'He has been raised from the dead' ...
Matthew 28.7 REB

There's a whisper in the darkness,
There's a whisper in the night,
There's a whisper in the dawning
And it's growing with the light,
The man on the cross
Who was dead
Is risen, and he lives!

There's a whisper all around us,
There's a whisper on the breeze,
There's a whisper in the rushes,
There's a whisper in the trees,
The man on the cross
Who was dead
Is risen, and he lives!

There's a whisper that is spreading
For the news has broken free,
Now the sound is growing louder
And it's news for you and me
That the man on the cross
Who was dead
Is risen, and he lives! HE LIVES!

From *A Song for East*

Risen Lord Jesus,
all our hope and confidence
is centred in you.
Through your life, death
and resurrection
you have blazed a trail
through life's perplexities
and opened up a path for us to God.
Travel with us as we journey;
lead us safely through
the snares and pitfalls which await us,
that at the end
we may reach the kingdom
which in this world
we have only glimpsed.

Easter Meditation

Christ was raised to life – the firstfruits of the harvest of the dead.
1 Corinthians 15.20 REB

To a woman mourning the death of her brother, Jesus said, 'I am the resurrection and the life. Whoever has faith in me shall live, even though he dies; and no one who lives and has faith in me shall ever die. Do you believe this?'

John 11.25-26 REB

To three grief-stricken women standing by an empty tomb at first light on the first day of a new week came the message, 'Do not be alarmed; you are looking for Jesus of Nazareth, who was crucified. He has been raised; he is not here ... he is going ahead of you.'

Mark 16.6-7 REB

Invited as a stranger needing shelter into a home at Emmaus, Jesus took bread, said the blessing, broke the bread and offered it to them. And they recognized him.

Luke 24.29-31

St Paul, knowing in his own life the power of the risen Lord wrote, 'Never give in then ... never admit defeat: keep on working at the Lord's work always, knowing that, in the Lord, you cannot be labouring in vain.'

1 Corinthians 15.58 JB

This is the command of the Risen Lord to his followers, 'Go, then, to all peoples everywhere and make them my disciples ... And I will be with you always, to the end of the age.'

Matthew 28.19-20 GNB

> **Lord, help us to know joy**
> **as a spring always welling up within us**
> **and give us the power to dance through life,**
> **not as men and women who are blind**
> **to sorrow, misery or shame,**
> **but as those who know your victory**
> **and who cannot but rejoice.**

From *Word Alive*

Do Not Cling

1st after Easter

'Do not cling to me,' said Jesus ...

John 20.17 REB

'Do not cling to me,' he said.
'Don't try to hold on
to yesterday's world,
it is past and gone.

'Don't linger by an empty tomb
hoping against hope
I might again appear there.
I am not to be found
in the past,
but in the present
and in the future.

'Do not cling to me.
I am no embalmed Lord
laid in an impressive mausoleum;
you can't visit my dead body,
but I can always surprise you
with my living presence.'

**If ever we come to a time
when our world has been so shattered
that we are tempted to retreat
into memories,
clutching such broken pieces
of the past as may be left;
speak to us, Lord.
As Mary heard so long ago,
let us also hear you saying
'Do not cling to me'.
Save us from looking longingly backwards;
teach us to seek you in the life
we must live today
and to expect to find you waiting
in the world of tomorrow,
knowing that we can utterly trust you,
whatever lies ahead.**

That Jesus Is!

1st
after
Easter

There were indeed many other signs that Jesus performed in the presence of his disciples, which are not recorded in this book. Those written here have been recorded in order that you may believe that Jesus is the Christ, the Son of God, and that through this faith you may have life by his name.

John 20.30-31 REB

That Jesus IS! No need to go further. This is the crux of the matter. If Jesus isn't, then scrub out all the hymns and the prayers, put the Bible into a museum and close down the churches. We either believe that he IS, or we make ourselves party to what in the end is nothing more nor less than a confidence trick.

That Jesus IS! Not that he once was. Not even that he did rise, but has long since departed into a heaven rapidly travelling away from us in an ever-expanding universe.

The Resurrection doesn't make evil any the less evil. A man or woman still stands helpless before brute force, before skilful manipulation of the law, before the machinations of warped and twisted minds, before deep-root-ed prejudice, pride or greed.

But the Resurrection – which remember is God's eternal answer, for God is unchanging – flings a shout of joy and of triumph in the face of evil.

> **When the voice has been silenced.**
> **When the face is no longer seen.**
> **When the body is no more than a heap of ash.**
> **When there is nothing left to shoot,**
> **hang, or crucify,**
> **the life, the love, and the truth**
> **are let loose**
> **and all the shootings,**
> **all the hangings**
> **and all the crucifixions in the world**
> **will not stifle them**
> **because Jesus IS!**
> **And this is our faith!**

Over To You

2nd after Easter

You died; and now your life lies hidden with Christ in God. When Christ, who is our life, is revealed, then you too will be revealed with him in glory.

Colossians 3.3-4 REI

Therefore, my dear friends, stand firm and immovable, and work for the Lo always, work without limit, since you know that in the Lord your labo cannot be lost.

1 Corinthians 15.58 R.

The play *Out Of This World* tells the resurrection story through the dreamli experiences of a political prisoner named MESSENGER who comes to faith in his ce Even as he makes his affirmation he is taken away to execution and for a mome the stage is empty. A PLAYER enters hesitantly. When (s)he speaks, the respon comes from four voices. The speakers are not seen.

PLAYER	Messenger is gone.
VOICES	It is the way of all, to live and to die. To die and to live. Whether we die the death of a martyr Or peacefully in our bed.
PLAYER	But Messenger is gone and the play is not ended.
VOICES	It is the way of the world that we must leave our work half done. Our tale half told. No one's life is complete in itself. At best we are but links in a chain.
PLAYER	But the audience is waiting. How do we end the play with no Messenger?
VOICES	You make his work your own. Become Messenger in his place. You end the play proclaiming that there is no end. Cry out that Christ is risen and wait for the response. Proclaim the end that is no ending.
PLAYER	*(A little hesitantly)* Christ is risen!
ALL VOICES	*(Quietly but confidently)* He is risen indeed!
PLAYER	*(More confidently)* Christ is risen!
ALL VOICES	*(Stronger)* He is risen indeed!

Over To You

VOICES   Now let it ring that all the world may hear,
Through doubt and disillusion,
Through greed and cynicism,
Through suffering, through pain,
Through evil and through death, let the cry ring:

PLAYER   *(Confidently and strongly)* Christ is risen!

The four voices are joined by others from all parts of the building who respond:

He is risen indeed! Amen!
Glory be to the Father
And to the Son
And to the Holy Ghost
As it was in the beginning
Is now and ever shall be
World without end. Amen!

Because You Are A Risen Lord

2nd after Easter

Christ is all, and is in all.

Colossians 3.11 REI

Because you are a risen Lord
we dare to believe
in life beyond death,
life which is the fulfilment
of the deepest longings of the heart.

Because you are a risen Lord
we dare to believe
that past failures
need not weigh us down;
that you free us from their burden
just as you freed your disciples
from the burden of their failures
at that first Easter.

Because you are a risen Lord
we dare to ask for renewed strength
to live our lives
with you
and for you,
starting afresh now!

Because you are a risen Lord
we dare to believe
that in you we may find
the only life that really matters;
the only life that endures.

Lord, live in us,
that we may live
as we have never lived before.
Let your life so flow through us
that we are freed from all
that is petty and mean
and may become the means
by which others also
learn to know you as a Living Lord
and knowing you, rejoice.

Upside-down And Inside-out

3rd after Easter

For in the one Spirit we were all brought into one body ... whether Jews or Greeks, slaves or free.

1 Corinthians 12.13 REB

Upside-down and inside-out,
That's what Easter's all about;
Death strikes hard, but life begins
Jesus, the defeated, wins.

All the majesty of state,
All the bitterness of hate,
Crucify him out of town
But they cannot pin him down.

Put to death in fearful pain
Jesus comes to life again,
Praying for his bitter foe,
'Lord forgive, they do not know'.

Upside-down and inside-out
That's what Easter's all about;
Love for hate and peace for war,
Sin and death can do no more –

Deaf shall hear, and blind shall see,
Dumb shall sing and lame go free,
Lost be found and hungry fed,
Christ is risen from the dead!

Faith renewed and hope reborn
In this resurrection dawn,
Upside-down and inside-out,
That's what Easter's all about.

From *A Song for Easter*

Upside-down And Inside-out

Glory be to you, God, Father Almighty,
Maker of heaven and earth,
of your faithfulness there is no end.
Glory be to you, Lord Jesus Christ,
Saviour of the world,
by your life and passion,
death and resurrection we are redeemed.
Glory be to you, Holy Spirit,
Lord and giver of life,
for you are with us to strengthen us
and lead us to the truth.
Holy and eternal God,
Father, Son and Holy Spirit,
we give praise and glory to you for ever and ever.

Slow To Learn, Reluctant To Follow

3rd after Easter

The command that Christ has given us is this: whoever loves God must love his brother also.

1 John 4.21 GNB

God our Father,
you have shown us
the way of life in Jesus,
but we confess with shame
that we have been slow to learn
and reluctant to follow him.
You have spoken
but we have not heeded;
your beauty has shone around us,
but we have been blind;
you have reached out to us
through other men and women,
but often we have failed to respond.

Forgive us
that so little of your love
has reached others through our living
and that we have sat so lightly
to wrongs and sufferings
that are not our own.

Forgive us
that we have harboured thoughts
that divide us from others.

Forgive us
the times when we have been
thoughtless in our judgements
and grudging in our forgiveness.

Forgive us
that we have been unwilling
to overcome evil with good
and that we have drawn back
from the cross.

> To all who confess their sins and resolve to live a new
> life Jesus says, 'Your sins are forgiven'. He also says,
> 'Follow me'.

Lord, may we truly accept
what you offer to us in your love,
be renewed by your presence with us
and grow daily in your ways.

Dying And Living

4th after Easter

So come to him, to the living stone which was rejected by men but chosen b
God ...

1 Peter 2.4 RE

'The good which I want to do, I fail to do', *(Romans 7.19 REB)*
that's the heart of it;
an inner conflict
where we win some
and lose some,
but lose far more than we win.
It's as though we had within us
a self-destruct button,
or rather,
a series of self-destruct buttons,
for we do our dying
by stages.

Left to ourselves
we would drift ever further from God,
ever further from life;
but in his amazing mercy
we are not left to ourselves;
Christ is in the struggle
with us
and for us,
and we may be reborn
again and again
during our earthly journey.

And when we do at last
cast off this body,
in Christ we may be
reborn,
resurrected,
to the life eternal.

Thanks be to God
for the gifts
in Christ
of forgiveness,
rebirth,
and resurrection
to eternal life.

Not The People
We Like To Think We Are

He is himself a sacrifice to atone for our sins ...

1 John 2.2 REB

God our Maker,
in the humiliation, the agony,
the absolute awfulness
of the cross of Jesus,
we see that your love for us
has no limits.
But such a love
is not comfortable for us to live with
for it makes us see ourselves
for what we really are.

We confess to you,
and to each other,
that we are not the people
we like to think we are.
We marvel that you know us
through and through
and yet can still love us.
Help us to trust that love
and to be more ready
to look for your guidance
in our daily living.

We also confess
the evil of the world
to which we contribute
and in which we share.
Forgive us that all too often
we shut our minds to the needs of others.
Forgive our reliance
on weapons of terror,
our discrimination against peoples
of different race or culture,
and our preoccupation with
our own material standards
and comforts.

Not The People
We Like To Think We Are

Forgive us Christians
for being so unsure of the Good News
and so hesitant in sharing it.
Raise us, we pray,
out of the paralysis of guilt
into the freedom and energy
of forgiven people,
through Jesus Christ our Saviour and Lord.

Grounds For Confidence

**5th
after
Easter**

*The Lord keeps faith, and he will strengthen you and guard you from the evil
one ...*

2 Thessalonians 3.3 REB

Lord Jesus Christ,
we rejoice in the promise
that you will be with us
in whatever lies ahead,
and that nothing can separate us
from your love.
When you shared our earthly life,
you brought to those who would receive you
hope, joy, renewal.
In amazement
men and women found that
God was present with them,
part of their everyday experience.
Lord, let this be true for us.
Surprise us, we pray,
open our eyes
to discern signs
that you are indeed present
in the secular world
which appears to have no room for you;
in all the days that lie before us,
may we both know you near
and delight to live as your people.

A Light Beyond The Darkness

For I am convinced that there is nothing in death or life, in the realm of spirit or superhuman powers, in the world as it is or the world as it shall be, in the forces of the universe, in heights or depths – nothing in all creation that can sep arate us from the love of God in Christ Jesus our Lord.   Romans 8.38-39 REB

A light beyond the darkness,
A joy beyond the pain,
A youth beyond the ageing,
A Lord who lives again –
    And dying isn't death,
    And failing isn't vain,
    The end is the beginning
    With the Lord who lives again.

A universe of wonder
And thought beyond the brain,
A love beyond the hating,
A Lord who lives again –
    And dying isn't death,
    And failing isn't vain,
    The end is the beginning
    With the Lord who lives again.

A health beyond the sickness,
Release from stress and strain,
A life beyond the dying,
A Lord who lives again –
    And dying isn't death,
    And failing isn't vain,
    The end is the beginning
    With the Lord who lives again.

From *Out Of This Worl*

**We would know your resurrection, Lord,
not merely as an historical fact
but as a present experience;
help us to take hold of it
with all our heart
and to live it with all our being.**

Down To Earth

Men of Galilee, why stand there looking up into the sky?

Acts 1.11 REB

We are to maintain the truth in a spirit of love; so shall we fully grow up into Christ.

Ephesians 4.15 REB

'Men of Galilee ...',
that brought them back to earth
with a jolt.
These last days
with their risen Lord
had seemed truly 'last days';
surely the kingdom
in all its glory
was imminent.

But no,
the time had come
to return to the everyday realities
of Galilee, Judaea,
and wherever else
on earth
their mission
might take them.

Men of Galilee,
why stand there looking up into the sky?
Have you still not realized
that you have work to do
and it is in meeting the demands
of everyday
earthly life
that your future service
to the kingdom lies?

Down To Earth

Though we cannot see you, Lord,
we know that we can
come to you in prayer
and seek guidance and strength.
Remind us, when we need reminding,
that it is just because
we would serve your kingdom
that we have to go out
and make our own responses
to the challenges that confront us
in the world we know,
the world in which
we must live our lives day by day.

The Mantle Of Elijah

6th
after
Easter
Ascension)

He picked up the cloak which had fallen from Elijah ...

2 Kings 2.13 REB

Safely dead,
the prophet may be honoured.
Those who feared him,
hated him
and hounded him in life,
now recognize his sterling worth;
admire his dedication to the truth;
his willingness to stand,
to live – to die
alone.

Safely dead,
the prophet may be honoured;
but woe to any who,
yet living,
assume the prophet's mantle.
They'll be denounced
as charlatans,
rabble-rousers,
and enemies of the truth.

Standing alone,
his master taken from him,
the young Elisha
knew the burden of the prophet.
Yet,
as a precious trophy,
he picked up the cloak
which had fallen from Elijah,
and striding boldly to the forbidding river
struck the water and cried,
'Where is the Lord, the God of Elijah?'

A new prophet was abroad in the land.

From *Prophets in Action*

To see the work that's waiting to be done,
to hear the call that bids me to the task,
to feel the strength that reaches out to me,
to answer 'Here I am' and so to go:
that I might so respond –
this is my prayer.

What Next?

Pentecost
They were all filled with the Holy Spirit ...

Acts 2.4 REB

Having been wanderers with Jesus,
they had dreamed of a day
when all would be settled,
ordered, secure.
Instead,
they were given the Spirit,
and the Calling.

The Spirit,
that they might
be channels of the life
they had experienced in Jesus.
The Calling,
to witness wherever
the Spirit should lead.

Would they become pioneers, adventurers;
or would they try to domesticate the Spirit?

Would they cling to the safe and the known;
or would they become children of Abraham –
risking everything
to follow the half-heard voice?

By the Grace of God
their mission became a voyage of discovery.
They found Christ
in Caesarea and Philippi,
in Ephesus and Rome,
always he was ahead of them,
waiting for them
to build new altars,
establish new fellowships.

Only the promise was secure.
Not the method, the structures, the rules,
the buildings or the institutions;
not the liturgy or the theology;
only the promise was secure.

What Next?

'Go!' said the Lord,
'Go as children of Abraham;
inherit the way of uncertainty
and of questioning;
yours is now the calling
to travel in hope and live by faith;
but be assured of this:
I will be with you always, to the end of time.'

Hear The Word Of The Lord

Pentecost

Can these bones live?

Ezekiel 37.3 REB

Surely it would be utterly useless
to speak of God,
to a people
so unwilling,
so unable to hear.

Their dreams had proved false,
their hopes had evaporated,
their ill-founded faith had been destroyed.
There was no spark left in them
to be fanned into a flame;
they were dead.

Dead!
So very, very dead!
Like the unburied bones
of warriors from an ancient battle,
picked clean by vultures,
bleached by wind and sun,
no sign of life left in them.

But the Word came –
'Prophesy!
Would you limit the Spirit's power?
Prophesy to these dry bones.
Prophesy!
Be faithful to your calling,
open the way for the Spirit
and even these dry bones shall live!'.

**If you should call us, Lord,
to work in a situation
we find totally discouraging;
to work in a situation
we are tempted to write off as hopeless;
open our eyes to its possibilities.
May we not distrust the power
of your Holy Spirit to bring life
even where we discern none,
and strengthen our will
to do what you would have us do,
and to do it with all our heart.**

108

Beyond The Formula

Holy, holy, holy is the Lord of Hosts: the whole earth is full of his glory.
Isaiah 6.3 REB

A cooling drink,
steam rising from the kettle,
a mountain stream,
Niagara, the Ganges,
a village pond;
waves breaking on the shore,
the ever-restless oceans,
frozen polar regions,
towering cumulus clouds,
a shower of rain.
All these are water,
signified by the formula H_2O;
but the formula
cannot begin to describe
the multi-faceted truth
of water in all its forms,
with all its life-giving properties.

So with the Trinity,
Three in One
and One in Three;
– a useful formula;
but beyond lies
the majesty, the wonder,
the power, the justice,
the creativity, the beauty,
the love and the rescuing –
the breath-taking otherness
that we so inadequately call
GOD.

Beyond The Formula

Blessed be God
who made the universe
and sustains and renews it by his power.
Blessed be Christ,
who lived, died and rose again
and who calls us to his service.
Blessed be the Holy Spirit,
teaching us the way of Jesus,
bursting into our lives today,
stirring and renewing the Church.
To the one God, Father, Son and Holy Spirit,
who reaches out to us in loving compassion,
be all honour and glory and praise.

Gloria

Love the Lord your God with all your heart and with all your soul and with all your strength.

Deuteronomy 6.5 REB

Glory be to you, O God,
for bringing order and beauty out of chaos;
for awakening within us a desire to know you;
and for setting longing within our hearts.

Glory be to you, O God,
for sending your Son, Jesus Christ,
to be born into this world
to live, to work, to suffer and to die among us
and to rise victorious over death.

Glory be to you, O God,
for your Holy Spirit working in our hearts,
witnessing to the way of truth,
drawing us ever closer to you.

Source of all life, truth and love,
Glory be to you, O God.

To An Unknown God

2nd after Pentecost

I noticed among other things an altar bearing the inscription 'To an Unknown God'.

Acts 17.23 REB

Undistinguished,
and unnoticed
by those who worshipped
more prominent, more fashionable idols,
stood an altar
TO AN UNKNOWN GOD.
This was first-century Athens,
but it could well have been
any place, any time;
for every age
has its seductive idols
and follows contemporary fancies
which leave a void,
waiting to be filled
by the God who for many is still unknown.

Samuel took a stone and set it up as a monument ...

1 Samuel 7.12 REB

Few trippers
came to see the rough-hewn stone.
The guide book had a solitary sentence,
'The Stone of Help
set up by Samuel with the words,
"To this point the Lord has helped us"'.
There was no need for
turnstile or tearoom:
sheep cropped the surrounding grass.
The weathered stone stood
half neglected, half forgotten;
yet some revered it,
to them it stood witness to past mercies,
a challenge to present living.

To An Unknown God

So stand churches in England;
soaring cathedrals
or squat village chapels;
'Stones of Help',
testifying,
'To this point the Lord has helped us'.
To this point – but tomorrow,
who can say?
Yet of this one thing
we may be sure;
it is not the Lord who changes.

From *Prophets in Action*

To Be Born Again

2nd after Pentecost

No one can see the kingdom of God unless he has been born again.

John 3.3 REB

A new-born child
is utterly dependent
on the one who supplies its needs.

A new born child
may well come
'trailing clouds of glory',
but there is no memory
to inhibit action;
no past to cast a shadow
over the future.

As that child
learns to use its senses,
all is wonder;
each shape, texture, colour, sound,
a new discovery,
each day's an age,
a simple room
the setting
for incredible adventures.

**Grant Lord,
that we may learn to trust
as the young child
trusts a caring parent.**

**Grant Lord,
that experiencing your forgiveness,
we may live each day as it comes,
unburdened by the past.**

**Grant Lord,
that we may ever
be open to new understanding,
and ready for new experience.**

**Grant that we too
may be born again.**

For The Right Use
Of The World's Wealth

Nor must you say to yourselves, 'My own strength and energy have gained me this wealth.' Remember the Lord your God ...
Deuteronomy 8.17-18 REB

Dig carefully now,
move with caution,
label accurately every find.
This was the market-place:
men bought and sold,
made and lost fortunes,
traded in merchandise
gathered from the four corners of the earth.

'Cargoes of gold and silver, precious stones and pearls, purple and scarlet cloth, silks and fine linens; all sorts of fragrant wood, and all kinds of objects made of ivory or of costly woods, bronze, iron, or marble; cinnamon and spice, incense, perfumes and frankincense; wine, oil, flour and wheat, cattle and sheep, horses, chariots, slaves, and human lives.
Revelation 18.12-13 REB

Why was this place abandoned?
Was it destroyed by fire and sword:
by earthquake, tidal wave, pollution or plague?
Did it die slowly over long years,
or in the lightning-flash of a nuclear explosion?

Sieve the earth carefully for the remnants of their riches.
Riches that might once have fed the hungry,
                              housed the homeless,
                              healed the sick,
                              brought learning to the neglected
                              and despised.

They were an intelligent, cultured and industrious people and yet ...

Alas, alas ... So much wealth laid waste in a moment.
Revelation 18.16-17 REB

**Lord, release us from our bondage to riches
and teach us to use our wealth rightly
lest it vanish
as it did at Sodom, Babylon and Hiroshima.**

Free Us For Service
(An Intercession)

3rd after Pentecost

You are salt to the world. And if salt becomes tasteless, how is its saltness to be restored?

Matthew 5.13 REB

All-seeing and ever-present God,
you know how we live
under the pressures of everyday life,
and how often we look at the world
from a very narrow and personal angle.

Help us now to open our hearts and minds
to the ways of the kingdom of our Lord;
that strange, dangerous, exciting kingdom,
which has a habit of turning
all values and judgements upside-down.

We pray for those who suffer the miseries of war,
and for those starving in a world of plenty.
We confess that the evil
in the hearts of men and women
which makes these things possible
is also in our own hearts.

Forgive us when we shut our ears to things
we don't want to know about;
and when we talk as though all the blame
for what is wrong in the world rests on others.

We pray for the Church.
Continue to break down the barriers
separating Christian from Christian;
and help us to grow closer together in love,
that the world outside our fellowships
may believe that your kingdom is indeed among us.

We pray for our families and friends.
May we grow in caring for one another,
and in awareness of those little signs
which tell us when those who are close to us
need extra understanding and support.

We remember loved ones who have died
and lift up to you those who are near to death.
We rejoice that you came to give us life
which not even death could destroy.
Lord, may this life indeed flow in us
and through us now and forever.

The Nature Of The Kingdom

You have come to Mount Zion, the city of the living God ...
Hebrews 12.22 REB

The kingdom
is a kingdom of wholeness,
and so it is at war
with everything that damages
and limits human lives.
It is at war
with everything that prevents men and women
realizing their full potential;
and so the kingdom challenges us
when we are content,
whilst failing to use all our powers.

The kingdom
is a kingdom of unlimited horizons,
and so it is at war
with all that sets bounds
and fixes limits
which are not recognized
by the Lord of the kingdom.

The kingdom
is a kingdom of willing citizens,
none are compelled to enter,
though all who accept its ways
are welcome –
and it is a kingdom
where those held in highest esteem
are not lords,
but servants.

In every age, Lord,
you seek for those who will hear the call
to become citizens of the kingdom,
to accept its responsibilities
and experience its joys.
Free us, we pray,
from all that hinders us
from responding freely and fully,
and in your mercy,
bring us at the end
to the city of the living God.

117

The Giver and Renewer Of Life
(An Intercession)

You are to rejoice ... and the aliens living among you, in all the good things which the Lord your God has bestowed on you ...

Deuteronomy 26.11 REB

If your brother has a grievance against you ... first go and make peace with your brother.

Matthew 5.23-24 RE

Eternal God, you have given us life
as you have given life to all peoples.
You call us into the Church,
that with men and women
of different race, colour and language,
different experiences
and different traditions,
we may be one body
to the glory of Christ on earth.
Help us to be what you have called us to be.

Creator of all that is, you give us wealth
in the earth and in the oceans,
forests and fertile plains,
air to breathe, water to drink
and all that is needful for human life.
We pray for those
who know little of your bounty,
for whom the earth is a cruel desert
and existence a constant struggle
against overwhelming odds.
We acknowledge that
the burdens of the poor
should be our burdens.
We acknowledge that we share
a common humanity.

Father, you have so made us
that we need one another,
but because we do not know
how to love everybody,
you tell us to start with the sister
or brother at our side.
We pray for those from whom we are estranged.
Bless them; and bless us in our future
relationships with them.

The Giver and Renewer Of Life
(An Intercession)

We pray for our families, our friends,
and all whom we meet day by day.
May they ever be conscious
of your love round about them,
and receive blessing
according to their particular needs.

You are present
in every part of human experience.
We hold before you:
    the infant in the mother's arms;
    children fast growing to maturity;
    young lovers planning their future together;
    men and women in the fullness of life;
    the sick and the infirm,
    battling with weakness and incapacity;
    and the dying, soon to experience
    your new creation.

We remember before you those dear to us
who have passed from this world.
As we received from you the gift of life,
so we pray that you will bring us
with them, to the life eternal.

The Time Of Testing

**5th
after
Pentecost**

For such a time as this.

Esther 4.14 REB

It was a time to keep your head down
and hope that trouble
would pass you by;
a dangerous time;
and she was young,
inexperienced,
and in a particularly exposed position.
True, she might possibly
be the instrument
of salvation for many,
but one false step
and her own life would be forfeit.
Was it fair
to lay such a burden
on a mere girl?

And yet,
might it not be
that the Almighty
had actually brought her to such a place,
for such a time as this?

And so Esther
took her life in her hands –
and acted!

**It may not be life and death choices
for us, Lord,
but difficult times do come,
times when we can be tempted
to opt out,
to say that the things that are happening
are no concern of ours.
Yet what if it *should* be our concern?
What if there is something
we should be doing?
Lord, whenever such need arises,
let your strength
enfold our weakness
that we fail you not
in the time of testing.**

Self-giving Love

Your people shall be my people, and your God my God ...

Ruth 1.16 RSV

She was not an Israelite,
her roots were in Moab;
yet Naomi
was determined to return to Israel,
and who would care for her
if Ruth did not?
It was a stark choice,
stay with her own people
and marry again;
or go with Naomi
into an uncertain future.
Yet Ruth showed no hesitation.
    'Where you go I will go,
    and where you lodge I will lodge;
    your people shall be my people,
    and your God my God;
    where you die I will die,
    and there will I be buried.
    Nothing but death shall divide us.'

And thus Ruth, the Moabitess,
came to Israel,
and in so doing
became an ancestress
of David the King
and of Jesus the Messiah.

    **Lord, you have told us
    that we must be ready to lose ourselves
    if we are to find ourselves;
    should we ever
    be faced with such a choice
    as confronted Ruth,
    give us grace
    that we may also choose
    the way indicated by
    a loving and compassionate heart.**

If The Gospel Possesses Us

6th after Pentecost

I am against those prophets, says the Lord, who deal in false dreams ...

Jeremiah 23.32 REE

If the Gospel possesses us, we shall not be able to help showing that v have loyalties to a kingdom with a radically different understanding what life is all about.

To those who worship the great financial director in the sky and who priests are stockbrokers and bankers, we shall be declaring the God wl pours out his riches for all.

To those who expect us to wheel out a tribal deity on special occasio to give credence to narrow national aims and prejudices, we shall l declaring the God whose love knows no boundaries and to whom eve woman and every man is dear.

To those consumed by ambition or greed, driven to climb higher or ama wealth without a thought for those they hurt in the process, we shall l declaring the God who calls us to life in community, where the joy strength is the ability to support the weak.

To those who see life in terms of aggressive confrontation, we shall l declaring the God who suffers and forgives, that he may bring his sca tered people back into one family.

To those who habitually use New-speak, calling retrogressive legislatic reform, who are not so much economical with the truth as deliberate camouflaging their actions with falsehoods, we shall be declaring the Gc who cannot be fooled by any public relations exercise, however brilliar ly it may be conceived.

At a time when successive Acts of Parliament are widening the alreac unacceptable divisions in our society, we will be witnessing to the clain of the God whose justice is concerned, not with statutes, but with rig dealing by the disadvantaged and who holds us responsible for the wa we treat our less fortunate sisters and brothers.

If the Gospel really possesses us, we shall show in our living a fellowsh in Christ of women and men who rejoice that they have a measure strength to help the weak, a measure of wealth to share with the poor, reservoir of love from which they may draw to refresh the unloved ar the rejected, and a passion for justice to confront the often squalid lega ity of our times.

Moderator's Address to URC Assembly, 19

For People Everywhere
(An Intercession)

I urge that petitions, prayers, intercessions, and thanksgivings be offered for everyone ...

1 Timothy 2.1 REB

Return, Israel, to the Lord your God ...

Hosea 14.1 REB

Lord our God,
we pray for the peoples of the world
of all nations and races,
languages and cultures;
we pray for them,
young and old, rich and poor.
We remember that today we ourselves
live in a multi-cultural society;
grant us understanding and tolerance;
help us truly to love those
whose way of looking at things
is vastly different from our own.

We pray for our children
and our children's children.
Teach us who live now
so to use what you have given
that we do not leave behind us a devastated planet,
that we do not leave stones instead of bread.

We pray for the men and women
amongst whom we live,
for those who share our home,
for our neighbours and friends,
and for those we meet
as we go about our day to day business.

We thank you for those we love
who make the world meaningful to us,
who bear with us in our follies
and who share
our hopes and fears,
our joys and sorrows.

For People Everywhere
(An Intercession)

Help us, Lord,
to see with your eyes
those for whom we feel little sympathy,
those we think we cannot love;
that we may also come to pray for them
in all sincerity.

We pray for those who are
in doubt or despair,
for those who are lonely
and those who are sad,
for those who are sick,
for those who are dying
and for those who watch with them.
Lord, may they know your peace,
that peace which passes human understanding.

You are a God of life:
enable us to know the life
which flows from you
in all its richness;
renew our sense of commitment
to one another;
break through the barriers we build
which could shut you out of our lives
and in your mercy
bring us at the last
to your kingdom
for Jesus Christ's sake.

Love Begets Love

**7th
after
Pentecost**

Her great love proves that her many sins have been forgiven ...
Luke 7.47 REB

Ever-living God,
you have shown the unlimited
love which you have for us
in the life,
death and resurrection
of Jesus Christ.

We thank you that the love
which flowed through him
has been working in the world
in every age
and that it still,
in our own time,
warms and transforms
the hearts of men and women.

We thank you that you not only
reach out to us
to forgive and heal,
but that you also call us to share
in the work of making your
love more widely known.

Let that love so work in us
and transform us,
that we may
live our lives
in ways that enable others
to come to know you
as you really are;
to experience
the reality of your forgiveness,
and the joy
of being set free by love
to live ever more lovingly.

Still You Call Us To Yourself

7th after Pentecost

Once more you will show us compassion and wash away our guilt ...
Micah 7.19 REB

Almighty God,
we worship and praise your holy name;
earth and heaven are full of your glory,
light and darkness are in your keeping,
and nothing is hidden from you.
You are the source of all life
and as we trust ourselves
to your loving kindness,
you strengthen and renew us.

You call us to yourself,
that we may be your people,
but the nearer we come to you,
the more conscious we are
of our follies and sins,
of our selfishness and our wilfulness.
We don't know where to turn.
And you tell us again
that Jesus came into the world
to save sinners –
    to accept us as we are;
    to forgive our past failures;
    to set us free from the grip of evil
    and to lead us in the way of life.

Now, in the quietness of our hearts,
we acknowledge our faults
and pray for forgiveness and renewal ...

When we truly seek him,
the Lord reaches out to us in his love
and says,
    'Your sins are forgiven,
    put them behind you;
    now, go out in my strength
    and live!'

126

A Matter Of Falling Out

8th after Pentecost

Euodia and Syntyche, I appeal to you both: agree together in the Lord.
Philippians 4.2 REB

Dwelling together
in heavenly concord
they sat in pleasant companionship,
each wrapped in her own thoughts,
until Syntyche broke the silence
by asking,
'Do you recall
when we were on earth,
that quarrel
which once shook the Church in Philippi?'

Euodia thought a while
'Yes I remember.'
she replied,
'At least,
I think I do.'

They were silent again,
each with a frown of concentration;
suddenly both spoke
as with one voice
and said, 'My dear,
whatever was it all about?'

**We will not always agree together,
in your Church, Lord,
but when we do disagree,
let it be with loving understanding
of one another's viewpoints;
and lead us from disagreement
into a deeper harmony
transcending all divisions,
that through your Grace working in us
we may indeed become one
now, in this world,
without waiting
for the harmony of the hereafter.**

When Faith Is Under Attack

8th after Pentecost

'How can I watch the child die?' she said, and sat there, weeping bitterly. God heard ...

Genesis 21.16-17 REB

I believe; help my unbelief.

Mark 9.24 RE[

Father, we have good times
and bad times;
we have times when all is bright,
and times when the shadows lengthen around us.
When the bad times come,
when we are troubled or distressed,
help us to become more aware of your presence.
Show us how to put aside anxiety,
and focus our minds
on what you would have us do.
You know how doubt and mistrust
can sap our energy
and undermine our will;
help us to overcome these enemies,
and strengthen our faith,
that we are indeed held secure
in the love you have shown to us
through Jesus Christ.

And when we *have* tried to do the work
which we believe
you have put into our hands,
grant us the confidence
that is able to leave
the outcome with you.

It Is Good To Be Still

9th after Pentecost

Come, let us return to the Lord. He has torn us, but he will heal us, he has wounded us, but he will bind up our wounds ...

Hosea 6.1 REB

The Lord said to him, 'Go back ...'

1 Kings 19.15 REB

And now
I can begin to forget
the turmoil,
the anxiety,
the sheer mental and physical exhaustion
of these past days.

How wonderful it is to be still;
to no longer have any responsibilities;
to be able to rediscover peace
and to know
that nothing else matters except
that you, Lord, are with me.

I begin to feel whole again.
Strength is returning.
You are very close to me now –
if only it could stay this way
for ever
and ever.

What is that you are saying?
Go back?
No Lord, surely not!
Go back?
'Go back, my Grace is all you need.'
Go back?

Yes, Lord, I do hear.
I have to tell you in all honesty
that I don't want to go back;
things won't be any better,
they might even be worse;
but,
if that really is your purpose for me,
then, strengthen my will
to follow wherever you may lead.

Yes, Lord,
I'm not keen,
but I'm going.

Help Us To Trust You

9th after Pentecost

You must go and announce the kingdom of God.

Luke 9.60 REB

Heavenly Father,
your love reaches out to us
each and every day of our lives,
and round about us the world
is full of your glory;
but sometimes we are blind,
sometimes we are deaf
and sometimes you seem very far away.

Help us to trust you,
especially when times are difficult.
Help us to see more clearly
the signs of your activity round about us.
Help us to hear more clearly
when your voice speaks deep in our hearts.
Help us, so that
with our sisters and brothers
all around the world
we may indeed worship you
with heart and soul and mind and strength.

Grant that this day
we may look to you as Father
and trust in you as Saviour,
that your Spirit
may live in us
and work through us
to the praise and glory
of your Holy Name.

The Patience Of God

10th after ntecost

'In forty days Nineveh will be overthrown!'

Jonah 3.4 REB

On the fortieth day,
Jonah made himself comfortable
and waited to see what manner of disaster
would overtake the city.
Dawn broke and gave way to morning,
morning to afternoon,
afternoon to evening.
Darkness fell,
and the people of Nineveh,
their day's work over, relaxed and rested.
But Jonah was angry, very angry indeed.

'Look here, Lord,' he said, 'as you well know
I didn't want to come to Nineveh
in the first place.
I had a feeling in my bones
that when I'd done all you said,
when I'd preached my heart out
and promised a first-class doom,
you'd spoil the whole thing by letting them off,
I mean, you're always doing that kind of thing,
you're notorious for it.
It's alright for you,
you're God,
you can afford to take a long view;
but it does take the heart out
of a good, honest prophet
just longing to see evil come to a sticky end.'

Patiently the Lord replied,
'Should I not be sorry for Nineveh,
with so very many people
who haven't got a clue
as to what life is all about,
but who yet might be saved?'

The Patience Of God

You have made yourself known to us
as a loving God, a rescuing God
and a God of infinite patience.
We come to you joyfully and thankfully,
yet we know that if we are truly to be your children,
something of your life must flow in us.
Give us grace to overcome any bitterness or malice
and to forgive those we may think have done us wrong,
that we may be able to receive
your forgiveness for our own faults
and enjoy the freedom
of those who belong to your family.

When The World Is Dark

**10th
after
Pentecost**

*Love in all sincerity ... Let hope keep you joyful; in trouble stand firm; persist
in prayer; contribute to the needs of God's people, and practise hospitality.
Call down blessings on your persecutors – blessings, not curses.*

Romans 12.9-14 REB

You will have no easy living
You must work for all you need
And then work to have some more
To give away;
If you find that you are angry
Don't you nurse it through the night,
For the Lord has shown to you
A better way.

When the world is dark
You must shine like stars;
When the world is false
You must be true;
When the world is greedy
You must give way,
And when the world is tired
You must renew.

You treat everybody fairly
Whether up or whether down,
Whether man or whether woman
Whether black or whether brown;
Watch your tongue when you are talking
There must be no room for spite
For the Lord would spread
No malice through the town.

When the world is lost
You must point the way;
When the world is sad
You mustn't mope;
When the world's adrift
You must keep on course
And when the world despairs
You give it hope.

From *Ragman*

**Left to ourselves, Lord, we should only fail miserably, but let your love
really flow through us and we may indeed shine like stars in a dark world.**

Faith In Action

Be ready for action ...

Luke 12.35 RE.

Lord of the ages,
you have shown us
that the heavenly vision
and the earthly task
are not in conflict,
but rather belong
each to the other.
Let not the busy-ness of our lives
prevent us from seeking
you in quiet retreat;
neither let our search
for signs of your presence
detract us from
the work which you have
for our hands to do.

Holy Father,
in whose hands lie our destiny
and the destiny of the whole of creation;
Lord Jesus Christ,
light of the world,
revealing the purposes of the Father;
Holy Spirit of truth,
bringing the knowledge of God
to our darkened minds;
Father, Son and Holy Spirit,
grant us to know
and to do your will.

The Things That Matter

11th after Pentecost

All the day long I have been made a laughing-stock; everyone ridicules me.
Jeremiah 20.7 REB

If the master has been called Beelzebul, how much more his household!
Matthew 10.25 REB

How shall you value the life of a man
How shall you tell its worth?
Shall you measure by skill, or by wealth or by fame,
By birth, or by breeding, or public acclaim?
No! For a life is the vision it sees
And the truth by which it lives.

How shall you measure the reign of a king
How shall you tell its worth?
Shall it be by the power of the sword in his hand,
The way his commands are obeyed in the land?
No! For a king is the vision he sees
And the truth by which he lives.

How shall you measure a prophet's word
How shall you know him true?
Shall it be by his voice and the glint of his eye,
A hand that he waves towards a far distant sky?
No! For a prophet's the vision he sees
And the truth by which he lives.

Then when a face has passed from your sight,
That person's no more to be seen,
Is their life written off with the stroke of a pen,
From dust now returned to the dust once again?
No! For a life is the vision it saw,
And the truth by which it lived.

From *The Battle*

The Christ Who Troubles Us

12th after Pentecost

Not on the Sabbath!

Luke 13.14 RE

> *I take no pleasure in your sacred ceremonies ... instead let justice flow on*
> *a river ...*
>
> *Amos 5.21,24 K*

This man he made the leper whole
He gave the blind their sight;
The deaf found they could hear again
To darkness he brought light;
And cripples found they had been healed
While silent lips became unsealed.

    But we are blind who will not see
    And lame who will not walk;
    And we are deaf who will not hear
    And dumb who will not talk;
    Captives, we do not seek release
    We do not want his way of peace.

To him the name of God was love,
His kingdom was for all;
The lost he welcomed home again,
The outcast heard his call.
To those who sought the promised day,
He was the life, the truth, the way.

    This man destroys our peace of mind
    We cannot bear his eyes;
    Just let us follow our own paths
    Don't point us to the skies.
    We want to walk in ancient ways
    Content and cosy all our days.

    We cannot bear the nonsense of
    A God for everyone.
    We'll serve the God who cares for us
    As we have always done.
    We dare not let this man go free,
    So nail him to the gallows tree.

From A Song For East

The Christ Who Troubles Us

Forgive us
the blindness of our eyes,
the deafness of our ears,
the rigidity of our minds,
and the hardness of our hearts;
and awaken us, Lord,
to our need for healing
and make us whole.

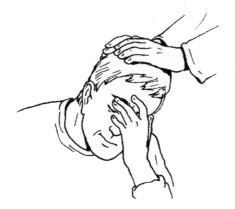

A Suitable Offering

12th after Pentecost

What shall I bring when I come before the Lord ... ?

Micah 6.6 RE

Isn't 'bringing' a little out of date?
I make an offering of course,
covenanted,
and paid by credit transfer;
the church receives a regular contribution
and I don't need to worry any further.
Other causes
I support by tax-efficient
Gift Aid
and,
while I don't altogether approve,
I'm still amazed
at how much can be raised
by a well-organized raffle,
or lottery ...

Money isn't everything?
No, I suppose it isn't,
though you won't get very far without it.
However, I'm in my place most Sundays,
well, quite often.
You must understand
I have a very busy life
with considerable responsibilities,
and I really don't see
what more can be required of me.

**Father,
in your son Jesus Christ
you have shown us
the true meaning of life.
Grant that we may be converted
and renewed in our minds,
so that we may know
that only in giving and spending ourselves
do we truly live.**

Not A Song For The Charts

All it yielded was a crop of wild grapes.

Isaiah 5.2 REB

Isaiah sings a ballad, but it is not what the people were expecting to hear. The song roundly condemns both their ways and their claim that God was behind them.

I haven't got a song for the charts
Not a song you'll be wanting to play,
Nothing to sing to feed your pride
Nothing to suit this day.
For the Lord isn't on your side,
He's not fighting against your foe,
His is the body you strike,
His is the blood that will flow.

I haven't got a word that you'll like
Not a word you'll be wanting to hear,
Nothing to say to stir your blood
Nothing to calm your fear.
For the Lord isn't on your side,
He's not fighting against your foe,
His is the body you strike,
His is the blood that will flow.

I haven't got a sign from your God
Not a sign you'll be wanting to see,
Nothing to show to cheer your heart
Nothing to fill you with glee.
For the Lord isn't on your side,
He's not fighting against your foe,
His is the body you strike,
His is the blood that will flow.

From *The Battle*

When we wilfully follow after our own
narrow, selfish purposes
and try to convince ourselves
and others
that we are doing your will;
forgive us, Lord,
make us aware of the evil we are doing,
and bring us to true repentance
and the reform of our ways.

Awareness Of God's Presence
(An Intercession)

13th after Pentecost

For none of us lives, and equally none of us dies, for himself alone.

Romans 14.7 RE

Heavenly Father, help us, that we may have
eyes to see beyond the obvious;
ears to hear, above a babel of sounds,
the still, small voice;
and hearts and minds alert
to respond to your presence,
even in the most unlikely situations.
Teach us to behave
as responsible citizens of your kingdom,
even when that behaviour
can appear quite irresponsible
in the eyes of others.

We bring to you those we would
especially remember at this time:
we hold in our thoughts ...
and we lift them up to you in love.

With deep thankfulness
for all we have experienced
of loving care in our own lives,
we pray for those
who know very little love.
We lift up those in trouble
who see no light
through their darkness,
who know no hope
to lift them above despair,
who long for inner peace
but feel that everything is falling apart.

140

Awareness Of God's Presence
(An Intercession)

Father, increase our awareness
and our sensitivity,
that we may be ready
to give more of ourselves
to those who most need our love.
Let your Spirit
work in us,
possess us,
and use us.
Fill up, we pray,
the inadequacies
of our asking and of our offering;
help us to trust you in all things
and to offer ourselves to you in all things,
for Christ our Lord's sake.

Conversation Piece

14th after Pentecost

And all the time the Lord went before them, by day a pillar of cloud to guid them on their journey, by night a pillar of fire ...

Exodus 13.21 RE.

Moses said to God, 'Go to Pharaoh?
No, not me Lord.
Just look what I'd be up against,
I really couldn't cope;
I've got settled in my ways
And I'm near to my retirement,
Me, go along to Pharaoh?
Why, I wouldn't have a hope.

'He's got the press on his side,
He's got TV, he's got radio,
The city and the unions,
(not often they agree);
He's got all the selfish fears
That bring the worst out in the best of us,
So what's the point of going?
Go on then, you tell me.'

But the word the Lord had spoken
By the bush in the wilderness,
Was a word that wouldn't leave him
It kept ringing in his head;
'There are slaves to be freed,
There are "write-offs" needing dignity;
There are homeless to be sheltered,
There are hungry to be fed;
And you're the one I'm calling
So it's time you set about it,
Don't stop to ask me how,
But I'll be there, so go ahead.'

Pharoah said to Moses, 'What's this nonsense?
I'm surprised at you,
I really looked for better things
Than all this "commie" talk;
I see when you were young
You were noted as a rebel;
If you want to get home safely,
I suggest you start to walk.

Conversation Piece

'What would happen to our trade?
What would happen to our industry?
The cost-of-living index
Would shoot up to the sky;
The madness you're suggesting
would wreck our whole economy,
of course I shan't release them,
I advise you not to try.'

Only a fool would have attempted it:
but he went ...
and it HAPPENED!

**There are times, Lord,
when you do ask
some pretty big things of folks.
Now I'm no hero,
I'm certainly not looking for trouble,
and I don't make much of a job
of the things you do ask me to do;
but if you do ever call me
to some fresh, demanding
form of action,
let it not be said that,
'He (she) never tried'.**

143

Skill To Distinguish
Good From Evil

Grant your servant, therefore, a heart with skill to listen ... and distingui
good from evil.

1 Kings 3.9 R.

Satan himself masquerades as an angel of light ...

2 Corinthians 11.14

How shall we,
who are engaged in conflict with ourselves,
engage for God
in conflict in the world?

Save us, Lord, from the foolhardiness
that imagines that it will
always recognize the enemy
and be able to distinguish
between good and evil
without the need to watch and pray.
Help us to discover where and what
you would have us fight;
give patience, where patience is necessary,
but bring us to action
where non-involvement would be sin.

Teach us to rejoice in the wild unpredictability
of your kingdom,
which defies every rubric,
can be programmed by no computer,
puts human beings
before convenient systems,
and grants citizenship
without regard for protocol or precedent.

Above all else,
let us be found engaged in your conflicts
all the days of our earthly life;
ready, when required,
to face the shame that is honour
and the defeat that is victory.

From *Prophets in Ac*

The People Of God
(An Intercession)

If you were Abraham's children ... you would do as Abraham did.

John 8.39 REB

God forbid that I should boast of anything but the cross of our Lord Jesus Christ ...

Galatians 6.14 REB

Lord of the ages,
you once called Abraham and Sarah
to set out into the unknown;
across the centuries you have called
other men and women to the same adventure;
today your call comes to us.
We do not hear clearly,
nor do we see clearly, yet we sense
that you mean us to be on the move.

The old certainties have gone
and by many messengers you tell us
that we have tarried too long.
Be with us as we travel.
Be known to us as we build
and rebuild our nomad altars,
so that once again your Church
may be a truly pilgrim people.

We acknowledge that you have called us
not to possess, but to give;
not to dominate, but to serve;
not to be elite, but to be true universalists;
not to be saved into an exclusive community,
but to work for the salvation of the world.

Teach us what it means
to be in the world and for the world
yet not of the world;
apart, but still belonging.

The People Of God
(An Intercession)

We thank you that within the world family
you have given us
a circle of closer relationships.
As Abraham and Sarah
took their many dependants
with them on their pilgrimage,
so we would bring to you
our family and friends.

We hold them before you in our prayers ...

We pray that you will so deal
with us and with them,
that we may not only be blessed,
but may in turn be blessing to others.

We pray for those we know to have
special needs at this time.

We especially pray for any without faith,
for whom life's journey
has neither purpose nor goal.

With joy and thanksgiving we remember
all those dear to us
who in their day ventured with you
and have now entered into
the city with firm foundations;
and we commend ourselves
and all for whom we pray
to you, the one true God,
who was, and who is, and who is to come.

An Enormous Gift

15th after ntecost

Presently there came a poor widow who dropped in two tiny coins ...
                                                        Mark 12.42 REB

Two tiny coins,
so small as to be
a nuisance to the banker;
yet an enormous amount
when recorded
in the ledgers of heaven.

When Jesus drew attention
to the gift,
the point, of course,
was not
that every little helps;
that God accepts an offering
however small.

It was not
that it was small,
but that it was given
at so great a cost.

Others gave far larger sums,
but they gave
what they could easily afford.
'She', said Jesus,
'with less than enough,
has given all that she had to live on.' *(Mark 12.44 REB)*

> **Only too well, Lord, you know**
> **how we use our money and our time,**
> **and how so often**
> **your service comes rather low**
> **on our list of priorities.**
> **You have given us so much,**
> **help us,**
> **so that with truly thankful hearts**
> **we may bring you**
> **offerings worthy of a God**
> **who for our sakes**
> **gave his all.**

The World's Poor

**16th
after
Pentecost**

There will never be any poor among you if only you obey the Lord your Go

Deuteronomy 15.4 RI

God loves a cheerful giver.

2 Corinthians 9.7

'You have the poor among you always',
said Jesus.
They did,
and we do!
Not, however,
by the will of God,
but by reason of human sinfulness.

'There will never be any poor among you
if only you obey the Lord your God.'
'If only',
there's the rub;
even in ancient Israel,
few took seriously the calling
to become a responsible community
where the strong supported the weak
and those with much
shared with those who had little.

'God loves a cheerful giver',
so Paul appealed for generous giving;
not to maintain church buildings
or finance administration and ministry;
but to relieve the poverty
of people they had never seen,
whose only claim upon them
was that they were also
members of God's family.

**Show us Lord, the joy,
which may be found
in willing obedience to the law of love.
Help us to discover what it really means
to accept the responsibility
of being part of the family of God.
Strengthen our willingness
to share the good things that are ours
with those who have all too little,
and in so doing,
to share them with you.**

The Lost Son Turns Home

16th
after
ntecost

But while he was still a long way off his father saw him ...

Luke 15.20 REB

Friendless, humiliated, hungry;
with nothing but the clothes on his back
and those filthy and ragged,
he thought wistfully of the home
he had so eagerly left
when he had money in his pocket.
He realized he had been valued there,
he had been wanted,
loved.

There was no turning back the clock;
but if he buried his pride,
– and there wasn't much left to bury –
might he be accepted in some inferior position?
He couldn't expect
to be taken back into the family,
but to live with his father's servants
would be infinitely preferable
to this present existence.

It took a mighty effort
to actually start on the road back,
all the time dogged by the question,
however could he face his father?
Yet something kept him walking,
endlessly rehearsing
the apology he would offer.
At last, seeing the house in the distance,
he halted;
he dare not go on;
he couldn't face it ...

There's someone running towards him –
his father!
The carefully-prepared speech swept aside,
he is enfolded in the warmth of his father's welcome,
all is rejoicing,
the lost son has come home!

Such mighty love, that though we stray
And cause our Father needless pain,
Forgiveness reaches out to all
Who turn their faces home again.

Freedom And Law

**17th
after
Pentecost**

God spoke all these words ... (The Ten Commandments)

Exodus 20.1 RI

Christ was offered ... to bring salvation to those who eagerly await him.

Hebrews 9.28

Straying ever further from the path
they found themselves in boggy ground
and soon became trapped
in a filthy, stinking swamp.
Sinking ever deeper
they cried out frantically for help,
but heard only the echo of their own voices.

When hope was almost dead,
they saw a figure struggling towards them
dragging a rough-hewn baulk of timber.
'Grasp this,' he cried,
'Grasp it, don't let it go'.
And so he drew them clear
and set their feet on firm ground once again.

With injuries that told
their rescue had been costly,
their saviour asked,
'How came you here
in such a situation?
Did not my father
show you where the firm ground lay?'

Shamefaced the answer came,
'We wanted to be free,
to live our lives
unhampered by restricting rules.'

'Had you not realized,' he said,
'my father gave you map,
compass, and waymarks,
that you might walk without fear
and so be truly free?'

**Father, teach us to value
the law you have given us,
and to accept it's discipline;
that walking in your ways
we may come to learn
what freedom really means.**

150

The Childlike Heart

17th after Pentecost

Let the children come to me; do not try to stop them; for the kingdom of Heaven belongs to such as these.

Matthew 19.14 REB

Lord of the heavenly kingdom,
you know us through and through,
all our weaknesses,
our follies,
our sins;
yet you continue to bear with us.

We pray that your love
may indeed possess
and breathe new life into us;
we desperately need you,
even though there is a part of us
which fears your coming,
fears you will turn our living
inside-out and upside-down.

Create in us childlike hearts,
that we may trust you
in good and bad days alike.
Strengthen our resolve
to make your truth our guide,
and to be alert
for the promptings of the Spirit.
Show us the full measure of our need,
that we may pray
and look for your coming
with joyful anticipation,
eager hope,
and a readiness to be changed.

Wrestling In The Dark

18th after Pentecost

Jacob was left alone, and a man wrestled with him there till daybreak.
Genesis 32.24 REB

Jacob is now a successful man who has not only outsmarted all with whom
has had dealings, but has also apparently come to a highly satisfactory accord wi
the Almighty (Genesis 28.20-21). He is on his way back to the land of his bir
intending with his wealth to buy off any remaining anger of his brother Esa
Everything is going his way when suddenly he finds himself involved in a lone
and desperate struggle with something or someone unknown. For the second tim
another world has broken into the experience of this out and out materialist an
when the struggle is over, it leaves him a changed man.

We have to admit, Lord,
that however much we organize our lives,
we are not the confident people
we like to appear
in the sight of others.
There are times when we, like Jacob,
must wrestle in the dark night of the soul
with forces that threaten to overwhelm us.

It may be blind panic,
a surge of despair,
or a growing, stifling gloom;
strength drains away
and it seems
life no longer
has meaning or purpose.

Are we to believe
that you might be with us in our wrestling;
that in this seemingly primeval spirit
which threatens to destroy us
you are at work,
wrestling with us and for us;
wrestling to reach,
beneath our 20th century veneer,
a truer, better self?

**Our prayer, Lord, is that you will indeed
be with us in all our inner wrestlings.
Save us from being immobilized by fears
or overwhelmed by doubts,
but contend with us and for us
that we may grow
closer to what you would have us be.**

152

A Fair Wage For A Fair Day's Work?

18th after Pentecost

Take your pay and go home. I choose to give the last man the same as you.
Matthew 20.14 REB

Schooled to be competitive,
we unquestioningly accept
the need for graduated rewards
to provide incentive,
and we can become very troubled
about differentials.

But in the Kingdom
there is only one reward,
and God does not weigh that out
in parcels of varying size.
In the Kingdom
to be employed is reward enough,
and it is sorrow
to stand idle in the market-place.
God's service
is not some forbidding task
to be undertaken
in the hope of joy hereafter,
and any who declare his service grim
must inadvertently
have engaged themselves
to some other master.

We acknowledge you as Master,
but if we served you solely
for some heavenly pay-packet
which alone should make work bearable,
how awful life would be;
how often we should be totting up our accounts
and trying to falsify the debit items.
But praise be, that is not the way of it.
With you there is no last or first.
In your Grace none will be underpaid
and most of us will know
that we have been blessed
past all deserving.

Idolatry

**19th
after
Pentecost**

*They have lost no time in turning aside from the way ... and cast for them-
selves a metal image of a bull-calf ...*

Exodus 32.8 REB

Not bull calves,
not today, Lord,
we wouldn't be so stupid.

But maybe a motor car –
our eyes caught by the advertisement
for that latest sleek, shining model,
the advertisement which suggests
it might also be the gateway
to many other delights.

But in any case,
what need have we
for the Word of the Lord,
when we have multi-channelled
radio and television
and a surfeit of daily papers?

What need have we for prayer
when we have the mobile 'phone,
and our every need
can be supplied
by the silicone chip?

And yet –
somewhere there seems to be
a loose connection.
We have more goods than we can use,
yet lack satisfaction.
We can circle the globe with ease,
yet lack direction.

**Lord, forgive us our idolatry;
make us aware of its dangers
and help us to look beyond
the material which perishes
to the eternal which endures.
Help us to recognize
the hype and the glamour
for what it is,
and bring us back to yourself
that we may rediscover
the true source of life.**

A Heavenly Citizens' Charter

19th after Pentecost

We are servants and deserve no credit; we have only done our duty.
Luke 17.10 REB

You've heard of the Citizens' Charter,
have you Lord?
But of course you have,
you hear everything.
So what about it,
is there going to be
a Citizens' Charter
for the Kingdom of Heaven?

I hope you don't mind my asking,
but these days
we are encouraged
to look to our rights
and to take care
that they are not neglected.

After all,
it's a bit old-fashioned,
this calling us to service
and reminding us of duty.
These concepts
don't count for all that much
in today's world.

And yet –

There's this odd testimony
of Christians over centuries,
that it was when
they committed themselves to your service
that they discovered what freedom really meant.

> **This is our prayer,**
> **to you our Lord,**
> **that you will show to us again**
> **the way of liberating duty,**
> **that, in commitment to your service,**
> **we may indeed discover perfect freedom.**

Privileged People

20th after Pentecost

I have great affection for you, knowing that, both while I am kept in prison and when I am called on to defend the truth of the gospel, you all share in this privilege of mine.

Philippians 1.7 REB

Strange privilege indeed,
to be writing from prison,
with a capital charge
hanging over his head.
Strange privilege
to have suffered
other imprisonments,
beatings,
mob violence,
and the bitter enmity
of his own people.
All this because
the Almighty
had called and commissioned him
to proclaim
far and wide
the gospel of the risen Lord!

**Loving God,
help us to understand this mystery
of being privileged.**

**Privileged, not to have,
but to give.**

**Privileged, not in that we are protected
against sorrow and pain,
but that we are promised
that you will be with us
and give us strength to face them when they come.**

**Privileged in that we are set free to love
because we know ourselves securely held in love.**

**Privileged to share in the work of the kingdom
and be numbered amongst all God's people,
the communion of saints.**

**Help us to understand this mystery
and to rejoice that we too
are called to be privileged people.**

A God Who Saves?

20th after Pentecost

If there is a god who is able to save us from the blazing furnace, it is our God whom we serve; he will deliver us from your majesty's power. But if not ...
Daniel 3.17-18 REB

'But if not'!
That's the crux of the matter.
What if there is no deliverance?

Some indeed come safely through the fires
kindled by hatred, bitterness, fear,
and every other motive
which leads to cruelty and oppression;
but many don't,
and die
in their thousands
and tens of thousands.

Are you indeed a God who saves?
What answer can we give
to those who cry
'How long, O Lord, how long?'

Was it not three men whom we threw bound into the fire? ... I can see four ... unharmed; and the fourth looks like a god.
Daniel 3.24-25 REB

God of all times and all people,
we praise you for the knowledge,
spelled out for us
in our Lord Jesus Christ,
that whatever troubles we may have to face,
you will never leave us to face them alone.
In Jesus we see
that you have made the sufferings of the world
your own sufferings;
that whatever fires we may have to pass through,
you will be there with us
and though we die to this world,
as indeed we all must,
you will still be with us
to lead us into the new life
of the world hereafter.

Jephthah's Daughter

21st after Pentecost

I have made a vow to the Lord and I cannot go back on it.

Judges 11.35 REB

And what it is that the Lord requires of you: only to act justly, to love loyalty, to walk humbly with your God.

Micah 6.8 REB

Jephthah speaks:

Son of a prostitute,
and driven from my father's house in Gilead,
I became a warrior.
The years passed.
Then Gilead required a warrior
to deliver them from Ammon,
and came to me.
I had learned my trade well
and, with the aid of the God of Hosts,
I led them to victory.

When Ammon threatened once again
I sought the Lord and made a solemn vow.
'Grant me this second victory', I said,
'and name your own sacrifice;
whatever greets me first on my return,
be it sheep, goat, ox, whate'er you will' ...
I did not think he would require my daughter.

The God of Hosts keeps faith
and I must keep faith with him;
but oh, that God could feel
the pain of a father
who must sacrifice his only child.

**Compassionate God, we grieve for all
who like Jephthah,
know nothing of your loving self-giving
revealed to us in Jesus Christ our Lord.
You are a Lord not of destruction
but of creation,
and whatever we freely offer to you
is not lost, but enriched,
touched by the glory of your kingdom.
Help us to share this truth
with those whose lives are darkened
because it is still hidden from them,
that they too may come to know
themselves held in your loving care.**

One Man To Die

21st after Pentecost

It is more to your interest that one man should die for the people, than that the whole nation should be destroyed.

John 11.50 REB

Caiaphas did not realize
that behind his cynicism
lay a deeper truth.
His intention
was to persuade his colleagues
that a timely death
would provide the solution
to a problem which threatened
both their comfort and their security.
For that he was more than willing
to sacrifice the life
of a young teacher
whose words and actions
made him feel distinctly uncomfortable.

Jesus would indeed
die for others;
but of his own will,
through his own determination
to follow the way of love
to the very end,
that he might
'gather together the scattered children of God.'

> **God of infinite patience,**
> **we marvel at the way in which you can take**
> **the cynicism and political expediency of Caiaphas,**
> **the treachery of Judas,**
> **the denial of Peter,**
> **and all the blindness, weakness, and folly**
> **of your people through the ages,**
> **and weave even these darkest shades**
> **into the tapestry which reveals your eternal purposes.**
> **But you do not do this without cost.**
> **We praise and thank you for the fact**
> **that, through our Lord's acceptance**
> **of the way of the cross,**
> **the gulf between your holiness**
> **and our fallen humanity**
> **has been bridged**
> **for all times**
> **and for all peoples.**

Waiting On God

22nd after Pentecost

I am the Lord, and there is none other.

Isaiah 45.18 REB

Amid all
our feverish activity,
the drive to 'get things done',
the rush to 'be ready on time';
teach us the skills
of waiting,
of being quietly expectant,
of being among those
who look eagerly,
yet without undue impatience
for your coming.

Amid all
our bustle and excitement,
busy streets and crowded shops,
programmes not to be missed
on radio or television;
teach us the skills
of listening,
teach us to distinguish
beyond all the clamour
the sounds
of your coming.

Amid all
our inner restlessness,
the feeling that we mustn't relax,
that there is always
another task waiting to be done;
teach us the art
of stillness,
help us to discover
the inner peace
that brings renewal
amidst all our busy-ness,
that we may have time for you
at your coming.

The Sacred In The Secular

22nd after Pentecost

If only I could have a drink of water from the well by the gate at Bethlehem ... The heroic three made their way through the Philistine lines and drew water from the well ... But he refused to drink it, he poured it out to the Lord .
2 Samuel 23.15-16 REB

Soon it was gone,
sucked into the parched ground,
until no trace remained
of the water,
brought at such great risk,
from the well by the gate at Bethlehem.

Three men had staked their lives
to satisfy his longing,
and David poured it away!

It was neither madness
nor indifference,
but a sense of the holy.
This water
was too precious to be drunk
and so David offered
this priceless gift
back to the God
whose holiness
may sometimes be revealed
in acts of loving sacrifice.

Teach us to recognize the holy
in those actions of others
we could too easily take for granted.
In the daughter caring for aged parents,
the husband caring for an ailing wife,
the parents lovingly caring for a disabled child,
the neighbours regularly helping the house-bound.
Give us eyes to see that in these
and many other selfless actions,
the sacred is made known in the secular
and you are glorified.

Death, The Last Frontier

Last after Pentecost

He will destroy death for ever.

Isaiah 25.8 REB

It is not so much the death
as the dying
and the knowledge that all must die;
that in this earth nothing is permanent,
nothing endures,
that death itself is the only certainty.

We pray for the dying,
especially those who are distressed and fearful.
We pray for those who grieve and sorrow,
especially for those who sorrow without hope.

It is not so much the moment of separation,
as the long, long days which follow;
the void nothing can completely fill,
and the knowledge that there must be other separations,
that no man or woman may be depended upon for ever.

Is death then truly vanquished?
Separation only for a period?
Shall ends become beginnings?
Shall grief be swallowed up in joy?
Is the end not death, but life?

'The Lamb who is at the centre of the throne
will be their shepherd and will guide them
to springs of the water of life;
and God will wipe
every tear from their eyes.'

(Revelation 7.17 REB)

Enable us, Lord, to live fully and joyfully
all the days you give us on this earth,
and when the time comes that we must depart,
lead us in your loving mercy into LIFE.

162

The Heaven For Which We Dare To Hope

Last after Pentecost

God will wipe every tear from their eyes.

Revelation 7.17 REB

His servants shall worship him; they shall see him face to face ...
Revelation 22.3-4 REB

To hear clearly the voice
which for so long we have half-heard
through a barrier of jamming and interference,
wondering whether it were true
or whether we had dreamed it so:
to hear clearly the voice.

To feel the strength,
the strength which we had imagined to be weakness;
the strength which,
looking back,
we know to have held us and defended us:
to feel the strength.

To recognize the love
which patiently has dealt with us
in all our failures, weaknesses and sins;
the love which has held us in life
and from which no power on earth can separate us:
to recognize the love.

To be entrusted with a task –
we who have failed so often –
and to serve him:
to be entrusted with a task.

To see his face,
the face we have never seen
and yet to recognize him:
to see his face
and know that we are known:
to see his face.

This, Lord, is the heaven
for which we dare to hope,
not that we merit it,
but that your love is great.

Holy Is The Soil

Harvest

God will supply all your needs ...

Philippians 4.19 REB

The earth is the Lord's, and the fullness thereof; the world, and they that dwell therein.

Psalm 24.1 AV

Holy is the soil we walk on,
Holy everything that grows,
Holy all beneath the surface,
Holy every stream that flows.

We will stretch our minds for the joy of thinking,
Use our skills for the joy of making,
Care what we make for the joy of caring,
This is the way of the Lord.

We will learn to share for the joy of sharing,
Learn to serve for the joy of serving,
Learn to love for the joy of loving,
This is the way of the Lord.

We will sing to the Lord for the joy of singing,
Give to the Lord for the joy of giving,
Live for the Lord for the joy of living,
This is the way of the Lord.

Holy is the soil we walk on,
Holy everything that grows,
Holy all beneath the surface,
Holy every stream that flows.

From *The Maker Of Things*

Lord, may we
never lose our sense of awe and wonder,
never take the miracles of creation for granted,
and never lose our awareness
that we walk each step on holy ground
and live each day by your Grace.

The Riches Of The Earth

Harvest

You will always be rich enough to be generous.

2 Corinthians 9.11 REB

Generous and loving God,
as we celebrate this time of harvest
we thank you for the beauty
and the fruitfulness
of the land in which we live.

We thank you for the wonders of the natural world,
the wide variety of its harvests
and the riches we enjoy
which come to us from other countries.

We thank you that we need never
go hungry or thirsty,
not knowing where to turn for food or drink.

We receive so many blessings,
save us from taking your gifts for granted;
stimulate our concern
for your needy peoples
who starve in a world of plenty,
and guide us, that we may be stewards,
not squanderers of creation.

We ask you to forgive us the damage
we have done, knowingly or unknowingly,
to this world in which you have placed us.

We ask you to forgive us the injuries
we have inflicted, knowingly or unknowingly
on the other creatures which you have made
to share this planet.

We ask you to forgive us
the ill we have done, knowingly or unknowingly,
to other human beings,
our brothers and sisters in Christ.

Help us to grow in caring awareness,
loving concern and instinctive generosity;
that we may praise you, not only in words,
but in deeds which enable others
to better share the abundant riches
you have showered upon us.

Index by Subject

Index Of First Lines

Index Of First Lines

Index Of First Lines

Index Of Biblical References